52
WAYS TO
HELP YOUR
KIDS DEAL
WITH FEAR
and feel secure

Jan D

OLIVER
NELSON

Thomas Nelson Publishers
Nashville

To
Dad
with thanksgiving that you
have always made me feel secure
in your love
and
have always taught me to trust
ultimately in our heavenly Father

Published in Nashville, Tennessee, by Oliver-Nelson Books, a division of Thomas Nelson, Inc., Publishers, and distributed in Canada by Word Communications, Ltd., Richmond, British Columbia.

The Bible version used in this publication is THE NEW KING JAMES VERSION. Copyright © 1979, 1980, 1982, Thomas Nelson, Inc., Publishers.

Printed in the United States of America.

Library of Congress Cataloging-in-Publication Data
Dargatz, Jan Lynette.
    52 ways to help your kids deal with fear and feel secure / Jan Dargatz.
        p.   cm.
    ISBN 0-8407-9405-3 (pbk.)
    1. Fear in children.   2. Security (Psychology) in children.   3. Child rearing.   I. Title.   II. Title: Fifty-two ways to help your kids deal with fear and feel secure.
BF723.F4D37   1994
649′.1—dc20
                                                        93-31639
                                                        CIP

1   2   3   4   5   6   —   99   98   97   96   95   94

☾ Contents

Sealing the Feeling of Security

☾ Introduction: The World Is Sometimes a Scary Place

The child's world is a world of experimentation, of testing boundaries and exploring potential.

The process is a lot like that used in chemistry class.

Do you recall the procedure for testing unknown compounds? A positive test result points you in a direction. You do further tests. Ultimately, the unknown becomes a known compound (assuming all tests yield accurate results), and you, the experimenter, discover certain principles about chemistry along the way. The same happens in life.

The difference between chemistry class and life, however, is that life is usually more scary and the principles are sometimes much more vague.

Many adults fear the unknown, even when they know their fears are irrational. Imagine the same unknown world from a child's perspective. Sometimes the unknowns of life are exciting. Sometimes they're ordinary. But sometimes they're scary.

Furthermore, from a child's perspective, most of the world is an unknown. A child begins from scratch in learning how things work, what the norms are, which protocols are appropriate, when certain behaviors are warranted, who is in control, and what is to be approached positively or negatively.

As adults, we have the tendency to dismiss a child's fears.

It's nothing, we say. Ah, but it is something to the child.

It's not real, we say. But to the child it is.

You'll grow out of it, we say. True—but only with information gained didactically or experientially. The three best antidotes for fear are these:

1. Information.
2. Graduated experience. This experience is controlled and begins from an experience that might be classified as "least threatening" and moves gradually, step-by-step, toward an experience that might be classified as "most threatening."
3. The presence of an ally.

Most of the ideas in this book are aimed at alleviating a child's fears and helping a child to feel more secure by providing information or by providing experiences that are guarded, guided, and graduated.

But first, a brief exploration of the four things most likely to provide a strong sense of security for your child.

1 ☾ Your Presence

You are the most real thing your child knows. Even a very young child knows certain things about the loving adults who feed, shelter, and clothe him:

- Their appearance, even in shadow or dim light

- The sounds of their voices

- The scents of their bodies and the colognes, soaps, or powders they use

- The feel of their hands and arms

Physical Presence And assuming that the adult has a loving adult-child relationship with the child, the child comes to associate the physical presence of that adult with the security, provision, and strength she needs to compensate for her insecurity, lack, and weakness.

The more closely a loving adult relates to a child, the more the child knows the adult's

- moods.

- likes and dislikes.

- means of expressing pleasure and pain.

- values held as absolutes.

He discovers how to make the adult laugh, shift focus, and show affection. He tests the boundaries of the adult's patience and beliefs to make sure they are intact. And he takes comfort in knowing that the adult remains consistent, predictable and, above all, available.

How can you help your child feel secure?

Personally Available   By being present in her life—not only physically present, but emotionally and mentally present:

- Present to answer questions

- Present to respond to her expressions of emotion

- Present to listen to her ideas, concerns, and problems

Consider the child with a scraped knee who comes running to Mom or Dad. The fact that he comes to Mom or Dad says that Mom or Dad is considered a refuge. The fact that Mom's kiss or Dad's hug can "make it well" is a testament to the fact that Mom or Dad is regarded as a healing, comforting presence.

The same mechanism is at work when a child seeks out Mom or Dad—or any other loving adult —after a piano recital, at the end of the school day, or before the kickoff of the soccer match.

The child who finds Mom or Dad, and who finds Mom or Dad willing and eager to be found, is a child who feels secure.

The most important thing you can do to help your child feel secure in a scary world is to *be there* when she needs you and to *be there* even when she thinks she doesn't.

2 ⸁ Your Touch

Your child needs to feel you and to be touched by you.

An Ever-Present Need Watch a young child in action! Watch him as he explores the adults he is coming to trust and love. He pushes their noses, pokes their eyes, pulls their ears, snuggles against them, and prods and probes until he is thoroughly convinced that he knows the feel and boundaries of his refuges.

In return, the young child giggles when nuzzled, sighs when cuddled, and relaxes deeply when held closely (even if for just a few moments before she is off to explore something new). She comes to know that the touch of a hand and the embrace of arms mean comfort, warmth, love, and safety.

A loving adult's touches, kisses, and hugs form primal memories in an infant. The need for the expressions of love and safety is never fully outgrown.

Active Affection Your child feels more secure when you

- hold his hand as you walk through a crowd.

- give her a one-armed shoulder embrace when you're standing together in a crowded room.

- gently stroke his head or brow when he is troubled or sad.

- hold her on your lap when she is sick.

- pull him close when he needs reassurance.

- hold her face when she cries as you seek an explanation for the tears.

- pat him on the back or shoulder before he leaves you.

- welcome her back into your presence (after an absence) with a hug, kiss, or gimme-five handshake.

Your affectionate touch says to your child, "This is someone to whom I'm connected and with whom I'm safe."

The safest place a child knows is the lap of an adult who loves him and who has arms wrapped tightly around him.

3 ‹ Your Voice

A young child can hear the voice or the whistle of an adult who loves him

- even in the middle of the night.

- even above the howl of a storm.

- even in a crowded noisy room.

- even over the din of an amusement park.

- even across hundreds of yards of wilderness.

- even into the blackness of a comatose state.

If you don't have a distinctive whistle for your child, you may want to create one. A whistle can call to a child who is lost, or who is on the verge of being lost, in a way that the speaking voice can't.

Speak to your child in a calm, reassuring, loving tone of voice especially when

- she expresses worry.

- he shows fear.

- she seems apprehensive about leaving your side.

- he finds himself in danger.

The best way to keep a child from panic, and the paralysis that can sometimes result from panic, is to speak to your child firmly, lovingly, and directly.

Use Your Child's Name Speak to your child by name. Call her name in your prayer times together. Kiss him and say good night, using his name. Call to her by name.

Sing, Too Sing to your child—even if you don't have the greatest voice in the world. Your child will value the song sung just for him. Your gentle bedtime songs will make dreamland a safer place for her to visit. Make up a song just for your child.

Speak Across the Miles The child who comes to know and value the voice of a loving adult draws comfort and meaning from long-distance phone calls. When you are away, be sure to call your child frequently and regularly—with frequency and regularity that are meaningful to her. The sound of your voice will help your child feel more secure, even though you are physically miles away. She'll know that you know where she is and that you care enough to make contact.

Your voice *is* the sound of safety to your child.

4 ☾ Your Guidance

A loving parent or guardian is a child's number one teacher. Your child will model your behavior—even if you don't want her to—so make sure you do what you want to see again!

Direct Guidance Your direct guidance can help your child feel secure in six ways.

1. Answer your child's questions Take time to answer your child's sincere questions as completely as your child wants them answered. (Your child will let you know if you are telling him too much—he'll lose interest in what you are saying. Your child will let you know if you are telling her too little—she'll ask another question.) Asking questions is the way your child learns how his world works and what things mean.

2. Clearly state what you want This advice applies especially in terms of behavior from the child. Don't just say, "Be good." State specific behaviors: "Sit right here and don't talk," or "Take two cookies and then go outside to eat them." Your child will feel much more secure in social situations if you will let her know in advance what is appropriate behavior and what will be punished as inappropriate.

3. Give your child options   Don't ask your child, "What do you want for lunch?" The options are too numerous for a young child to encompass. He'll feel far more secure if you ask, "Do you want a turkey sandwich or a peanut butter sandwich for lunch?" Children *want* boundaries in which to move and to make decisions.

4. Make suggestions   Give your child ideas about what to do or say. "Here's the way I make a new friend . . ." is advice that can help your child feel secure as she goes to preschool or school. If you are visiting an unfamiliar church, you might want to suggest, "While you're sitting here quietly in church, you might want to look closely at the stained glass windows. See what you can see." Your child will feel more comfortable in his new surroundings if he has a clue or two about what to do.

5. Give your child a preview   Let your child know what she can expect, the rules that are going to be followed, and the protocol that must be kept. Even if you are just going to the grocery store, give your child an idea about how long you are going to be there, what you are going to buy (and not buy), and what your child can do to help you in the process. Tell him what to expect as he faces going to a new school, joining a new group, playing on a new team, or competing or performing for the first time. The more you let your child know what she can expect, the more confident and secure she'll feel facing a new environment, a new group, or a new procedure.

6. *Be consistent in your guidance*   Don't offer Advice A or Expectations A on one day, and then reverse your guidance the next. If you discover that you have erred in the information you have given, own up to the error and give your child the correct information as quickly as possible.

Patience   Be patient in providing guidance to your child. You may need to tell again, explain anew, or answer a question another time. If your child repeatedly asks questions you have already answered or asks for more details, he may be sending you a signal that he isn't quite sure what you want, what is appropriate, or what is meant, and if that is the case, he is feeling insecure.

Assure your child that you will answer her questions or give her advice to the best of your ability, but that you sometimes make mistakes. If that turns out to be the case, admit your mistake and apologize to your child. You'll only add to her sense of insecurity if she believes she has failed for reasons she doesn't comprehend.

5 (Light

The dark is a scary place to most children—and to most adults, too! From the earliest stories we tell to our children and were told ourselves, the dark is the place where evil abounds, where monsters live, and where danger lurks.

The antidote for darkness, of course, is light!

Monsters are allergic to light—or so the parental advice might go. Dangers can be spotted when an area is lit.

A Night Light A small night light in a child's room, in hallways of the home, and in the bathroom that the child uses can give your child reassurance that she can find her way in the darkness.

A Flashlight Every child beyond the age of five should have a flashlight of his own. A flashlight is an indispensable tool in battling the images and fears of darkness, whether at a campsite or in his bedroom. Give your child permission to use it whenever and wherever he desires.

Control Over the Lights   Don't insist that all lights be out if your child asks for them to be left on. You can always turn them off after your child is asleep. Provide a small lamp next to her bed so she can turn it on if she needs it.

If your child is coming home from school to an empty house, give him permission to turn on as many lights as he wants. Lights can make the home-alone child feel more secure and also lift his spirits. (Turn on lots of lights during rainy days. Everybody will feel a little more cheerful.)

Make sure your house has adequate outside lighting—perhaps floodlights and certainly adequate porch lights and walkway lighting. If your child is home alone, she should be given permission to turn on the outside lights as soon as it begins to get dark.

Excursions into the Darkness   Periodically take a walk with your child in the night. It may be around the block in your neighborhood (assuming that it is safe to do so). It may be a walk in the woods on a moonlit night. Let your child experience the magic and mystery of night sounds and shadows.

6 ☾ The Familiar

We all know the value that Linus places on his blanket (in the *Peanuts* comic strip). Your child's security blanket may not be an actual blanket, but he likely has some toy, stuffed animal, or object that speaks to him of comfort, home, and safety. Allow your child to take that item with him whenever he is headed for a new environment.

As your child grows older, of course, she'll probably shift her security feelings to objects that are smaller or to various objects from time to time. She may want to have something to carry in her wallet. It may even be a familiar piece of clothing, such as a cap or scarf.

Photos Even a young toddler enjoys having a wallet of his own with cards and photos in it. Give your child a photograph of you that he can frame and put in his room (and take with him in his suitcase to camp). How about choosing a photo in which you are holding your child close or playing with him?

A Special Gift   In some cases, a piece of jewelry—such as a necklace, bracelet, or ring that is worn virtually all the time—can be a tangible expression of Mom's or Dad's love, even across time and space. Such a piece of jewelry can be a very real symbol to a child that someone on the earth cares for her and is continually concerned about her. Give your child something that is meaningful but not necessarily expensive. That way, if she loses it, she won't feel as if she's violated the love behind the gift.

Pillow and Blanket   As you travel with a young child, take along his pillow and blanket from home. He'll feel more secure in a strange bed and hotel room or even more at home in an airline seat.

Moving Tips   If you are moving to a new house or to a new city, take something from the old house or neighborhood as a reminder of the good times you had there. It may be a scrap of wallpaper or a rock from the garden. You might even want to create a special shoe box of such items and label it "a time capsule from the past." Include photos of the old house (exterior and interior), neighborhood, and city. Choose items for the box that have a story. You might even want to take seeds or cuttings from bushes and plants at the old house to transplant to the new one. Such actions give your child a sense of continuity with the past and a feeling of enhanced security that the new place will soon feel like home.

7 ☾ Words of Joy

We all know the message of the song "Whistle a Happy Tune." But we tend to forget sometimes that songs and words of joy we sing to ourselves truly *can* make a difference in our level of courage and confidence.

Don't stifle your child's desire to talk to herself. Encourage it! Moreover, encourage your child to make up stories and dialogues about happy things, dealing with pleasant subjects, with strong, confident heroes, and with happy endings.

Songs   Teach your child happy songs that bring a smile to the face. Include praise choruses and spiritual songs that speak of God's sovereignty, power, and omnipresence.

Nonsense rhymes and tongue twisters can also avert a child's attention away from what is causing fear or uneasiness.

Morale Boosters   Urge your child to speak positive words of encouragement to himself. Listen closely to the way your child talks to himself on the playground. If he makes a mistake or falls down, does he say, "Stupid," or "Way to go, klutz"?

Or does he say, "Next time I'll get it right," or "I need to try that again"?

You won't always be around to cheer your child on. Train him to be his own best cheerleader.

The Value of Praise   Praise isn't the exclusive property of adults. Children can voice praise, too! Teach your child as many names and attributes of God that you can. Teach her to respond to her worries, fears, and crisis moments by saying, "I trust You, God, because You are my _____ (*name or attribute of God*)." Rehearse praise in good times so that the words are quickly on the lips of your child when trouble strikes.

8 ☾ Power over Monsters

Children today are bombarded with monsters, goblins, ghouls, and other scary creatures. If you doubt it, check out the children's section in your local library, Saturday morning television programs, or a children's toy store! Imaginary creatures abound, and many of them play the role of the bad guy in the fairy tales, comic books, and adventure stories in which they star.

In addition to having to cope with these monsters, children frequently fantasize about the unknown and give it faces and sounds. They frequently attribute mysterious shadows or unusual events to monsters or evil creatures.

Important Facts Parents need to recognize three important facts about monsters and the relationship children have to them:

First, to preschoolers, monsters and imaginary creatures tend to be "real." Children under the age of four have a poorly developed ability to differentiate between reality and fantasy.

Second, most young children have very active dream lives, and they tend to dream about what they see and experience during the day.

Third, young children tend to respond to the reality of their worlds emotionally, and very quickly.

Tips for Helping Your Child Cope   What, then, is the wise course to take in helping your child cope with monsters? Here are some tips:

Limit your child's excursions into fantasy   Turn off scary television programs. Whenever possible, review books, cartoons, and comic books before your young child sees them. Watch your child's reactions to stories he sees or hears. If he shows genuine fright, step in either to stop the story or to offer words of comfort. In limiting exposure to the weird, frightening, and ghastly, you'll be sparing your child countless nightmares.

Talk about monsters with your child   Discuss especially *your* feelings toward scary things. Your young child may not be convinced that monsters aren't real, but she can be convinced that you aren't frightened of them! Share with your child what you do when you are frightened or feel that you don't have control over a situation. When it comes to monsters, it's more important that your young child learn to deal with her fear than with the difference between reality and fantasy.

Help your child feel empowered   A child who feels empowered is a child who feels more secure. Sometimes leaving a light on serves as empowerment; sometimes teaching your child a song to sing or words to say gives him a tool to use before panic sets in.

Help your child develop the ability to turn the unknown into the known   Teach your child how to distinguish fact from fiction—for example, how to tell what is causing a shadow, how to discern where a noise is coming from, or how to identify strange shapes in the dark. Make exploration of the unknown an adventure. At the same time, help your child learn what should give her reason to sound an alarm.

Never make fun of your child for being afraid of monsters   Comfort your child. Don't offer logic when a hug is what your child really needs. There will be plenty of time to offer explanations or advice as your child grows older.

9 ☾ Clear Directions

One of the greatest allies your child can have against fear is information.

Boost Courage Children feel insecure and fearful when they don't know what to do, precisely where to go, how to behave, or what to expect. Arm your child with facts, reasons, and directions.

Give your child clear instructions Keep your directions and instructions simple and to the point. Use command statements, not questions. For example, say, "Be sure to wipe your shoes on the mat before walking into Grandma's house," rather than, "Now, you'll remember to wipe your shoes on the mat before going into Grandma's house, won't you?"

Ask your child to repeat your directions or instructions back to you You can do this in a gentle manner: "Now . . . let's see if Captain Belinda got her mission orders right. What is your mission, Captain Belinda?"

Enumerate your directions or instructions Say, "Here are three things I want you to do. Number one, make your bed. Number two, put your dirty clothes in the hamper. And number three, empty your wastepaper basket." Limit your instructions to three or four directives. A child can remember only so many things at a time! Whenever possible, use an acronym, rhyme, song, or picture to help your child remember key information.

Provide a map, and make sure your child knows how to read it   Don't just tell your child where the rest rooms are in the basement below the auditorium, draw him a little map to get there. Ask him to verbally walk through the map with you.

Put words into your child's mouth or at least into her mind   Don't say to your child, "Give our host your thanks." Instead, say, "Now is the time to go over to Mr. Bellman and say, 'Thank you for inviting me. I had a nice time.'"

Anticipate the results   Rehearse with your child the appropriate responses in situations that your child might find new or awkward. Anticipate together what your child might say if he wins or if he loses. Discuss what your child might say when she greets her birthday party guests at the door or opens a gift, what to say to the child who is mean to her on the playground, or what to say when the teacher calls on her and she doesn't know the answer.

10 ᶜ A Way Out

Every place, and nearly every awkward or unpleasant situation in life, has a way out. Teach your child that principle by providing him with examples. A child who has confidence that he knows what to do in an emergency is a child who has more courage when an emergency occurs.

Quick Action Emphasize to your child the importance of taking quick action in an emergency. The first priority should be to leave the scene. "Get out and get help!" is a good rule of thumb to teach your child. The earlier she identifies an emergency, the better her chances of survival.

Emergency Escape Routes Your child needs to know how to

- get out of your house in case of fire.

- get out of his school in case of fire or other threat.

- find the emergency exits in a plane, boat, or train.

Map out an escape plan from your house with your child. Rehearse a fire drill in your home. Discuss which paths to take if certain exits are blocked. Talk to your child very specifically about the importance of her getting out of the house quickly and without looking for valuables or pets. Show your child how to walk or crawl low to the ground to avoid inhaling smoke. Impress upon your child the importance of *not* going back into a burning or smoke-filled building or house—*no matter what or why.*

Instruct your child how to talk to himself if he begins to panic—"Say over and over to yourself, 'Move, move, move' "—and what to say to others who may be experiencing panic—"Say calmly and many times, 'Keep calm. Keep going. Keep calm. Keep going.' "

Clearly Marked Exits When you are in buildings or vehicles, stadiums or amusement park "dark rides," periodically point out to your child the "Exit" signs. Instruct her to look for such signs as her first move in an emergency.

When in an elevator with your child, talk about what you would do if the elevator became stuck—indicate where the emergency buttons are located and explain the purpose of an in-elevator phone.

Social "Escapes" Your child should be given the freedom to leave socially awkward or dangerous situations, which may be just as damaging to his psyche as a physical emergency would be to his body.

Your child does not need to take taunts, ridicule, verbal abuse, or attacks against her personhood (including race, religion, and sex) from anybody. Make sure your child understands the difference between discipline and a personal attack. A personal attack is one that attempts to destroy your child's self-worth and self-identity on the basis of personal characteristics, not behavior. It's one thing for a coach to say, "You fumbled the ball. Don't do that in the future. Here's how to avoid fumbling." It's quite another for her to say, "You're always a fumbler and totally worthless as a player." The former is a part of good coaching. The latter is an unnecessary personal attack.

As in the case of physical danger, your child should leave a psychological or emotional crisis situation *as soon as he realizes what is happening* and as quickly and calmly as possible.

11 ⸫ Giving an OK to Comfort

Give your child permission to be comfortable. She'll feel a lot more secure in any environment.

Comfort in Clothing Dress your child in a way that allows for freedom of movement. Even "dress up" clothes can be loose fitting and easy to wear. Consider the child who is told, "Don't get dirty and don't get wrinkled, but have a good time!" It's simply not possible. Allow your child to get dirty in the course of normal play. Expect clothes to get crumpled. Choose clothes that stand up to wear and repeated washings.

If your child is worried about what he is wearing or is uncomfortable with what he is wearing, he can't possibly feel very secure in a situation. Feeling less secure, he's more likely to make mistakes that will cause the very spills or accidents you were hoping he would avoid!

Freedom of Behavior Within Limits
Give your child guidelines for behavior, and then let her feel free within those boundaries. The more freedom of behavior you allow your child *within boundaries,* the more secure she will feel in virtu-

ally any environment. She will know that it's OK to be human and to be herself, no matter who else is present.

For example, point out an area of the room, yard, or park where your child may play, and then let him play within that space. Or you might insist that your child be quiet during a meeting but give him the freedom to think, daydream, draw, color, read, build with blocks, or play silently. Or you might insist that your child stay next to you in the pew at church but then give her the freedom to work Bible-related puzzles, look through her picture Bible (or read it), gaze up at the stained glass windows, or curl up and sleep.

If your young child can see better by standing up on the chair (and is not blocking the view of a person directly behind him), let him take off his shoes and stand. The more your child is a participant in an event, the less bored and fidgety he is likely to be.

Natural Happenings Don't punish your child for natural physical behaviors, such as yawning, sneezing, or coughing. The child who suspects she will be punished for making any noise at all is going to be extremely uncomfortable during an event, and she will associate pain and discomfort with such an event in the future.

12 (Fitting In

The child who feels like the odd man out is going to be insecure and continually on guard against the taunts and teasing of others. Do your best to help your child fit in with his peers.

Wearing the Right Stuff You need not buy designer labels or the current fad clothing, but you should help your child dress within the bounds of current styles and long-range trends. Choose classic designs whenever possible—ones that will be in style from year to year.

Having the Right Stuff Again, you need not buy the hottest item for your child, but you should make certain that your child has what she needs, such as school supplies, lunch money, a backpack for carrying books, and a mitt for after-school practice.

Fixing the Flaw If your child needs a new hairstyle—or perhaps a more manageable one—take him to a professional. If he needs glasses, get them. If your child needs braces, do your best to provide them, too. A child's appearance is directly linked to his self-esteem.

Exhibiting Good Manners
Good manners are appropriate at all times and with all people. Teach your child how to say "please," "thank you," "I'm sorry," "I beg your pardon," and "excuse me" —not only with authority figures but with your family and with friends.

Building a Circle of Friends
Build a circle of friends for your child; make an effort to do so! Invite your child's friends into your home for a meal, a night over, a party, or an outing. Get to know your child's friends and have them get to know you as a loving parent and adult friend. If you are *not* involved in choosing your child's friends, you will be far less able to counteract the impact of the friends your child chooses for himself.

Spend time with your child and her friends. Watch how she interacts with others. If you need to help your child with social or communication skills, do so. Give advice about what to say or try, without ridiculing your child or manipulating her friendships.

Recognize that your child will always feel more secure at a party, social outing, or event if he has a friend with him. One child can get picked on by others; two children rarely suffer that fate, and if they do, they have each other as confidants.

13 (Reality Tests

Since much of what causes a child to feel insecure or fearful is illusionary—but nonetheless real to the child—a parent can provide training on how to separate fact from fiction and real danger from imagined danger.

Discuss "Stories" Watch television and movies *with* your child. Discuss afterward what was real and what wasn't. If you have an opportunity to take your child on a movie-studio tour, do so. Many children no doubt could say what a young tourist said: "It's just amazing how they can make you feel that it's real."

Reality Checklist You can help your child discern if something is real or an illusion by teaching him simple tests.

Does it move? The lint on the floor may look like a spider. Watch to see if it *moves*. If it does, and in a normal way, it's likely a living thing. If not, or if it's caught by the wind, it's probably inanimate.

Does it have a regular repeated pattern? The house will tend to creak a board here and a board there. Footsteps, on the other hand, are more rhythmic. The shutters or tree branches will tend to clap against the house in an erratic manner during a wind storm. A person tapping on the window pane will do so in an even manner.

Human behavior also tends to be consistent in one direction or other (toward evil or good) over a long period of time. Teach your child to watch for long-term trends. A person who is usually mean and then suddenly turns "nice" is a person to be regarded with suspicion. A nice person who without provocation suddenly turns "mean" is also someone to approach with caution.

Does it cast a shadow? Shadows don't cast shadows. Monsters don't have shadows. If it's real, it will cast a shadow. (And if it's dark, it will cast a shadow when a flashlight is aimed at it!)

Truth or Lie? You can also help your child determine if someone is telling the truth or a lie with simple tests.

Can it be verified? The Bible states that the truth is established by two or three witnesses. Look for someone else to tell the same story with the same details about time, place, appearance, actions, and/or sequence. The question to ask is, "Who else can tell me about this?"

Is there a threat attached to it?   Abusers frequently tell their victims, "Don't tell anyone. If you do, I'll hurt you (or hurt the other person)." Teach your child that such a threat is a sure sign of a lie. The truth is that the child is *already* hurt by such a statement and he *should* tell so the abuser can be stopped. Assure your child that your best defense against an abuser is for your child to tell you that someone is threatening to hurt you.

Ask, "Why are you telling me this?"   If your child suspects that someone is trying to manipulate her, spread false gossip, or play on her gullibility, this is one of the best questions she can ask. If she isn't satisfied with the answer, she should probe further. If the information is true and valuable and the motives of the teller are pure, the teller will give reasonable answers that are for the listener's good.

14 ☾ Locks and Keys

Your child will feel more secure if he knows that he can lock others out of his world—whether it is the bathroom, a diary, a bedroom, the house, or a clubhouse—and that he can gain access into his world when he wants it. Locks and keys are big security providers for children.

The Reason for Locks Your child will know that locks are for keeping people out. (She will have watched you use locks for that very purpose in keeping her out of your room or the bathroom!) You can *expect* your child to try to lock you out on occasion—and to take great delight in doing so. One mother of a toddler wears a necklace of keys to ensure that she can always get back into her house and her child's room.

Teach your child that locks within your home are for security against danger and that signs are for privacy. Give your child a "Do Not Disturb" sign for his bedroom door. Heed it when he uses it. He'll feel secure in his space without resorting to locks.

Unlocking Skills, Too Show your child at an early age how to *unlock* certain objects—especially a car door, the bathroom door, a stall in a public rest room, or a window. Such skills could be important to your child's safety or even survival in an emergency. (Make certain, of course, that your child knows never to unlock or open the door of a car in motion.)

Show your child how to use keys, and give her practice in manipulating them. Children love the privilege of opening doors, unlocking objects, and pushing code buttons.

Unlocked Hiding Places Children of all ages enjoy hiding—under a blanket, in a closet, under the bed and, unfortunately, in some places where they can inadvertently lock themselves in. Make certain that no empty refrigerators or freezers are lurking in your neighborhood and, if they are, that the handles have been removed from them so that no child can be locked inside. The same goes for large trunks and extra large suitcases.

A Key to the House You may not want your child to carry a house key, but you should let him know where a key is available (perhaps at a neighbor's house) so that he can let himself into your house if you aren't at home. Being locked out almost automatically results in a feeling of insecurity or fear. Teach your child to return the key immediately once he has used it so that it will be there if needed in the future.

15 ☾ Self-Defense Courses

Self-defense courses can be real courage builders for children who are afraid of personal attack.

Find a program that is

- geared to your child's age level. A six-year-old child's concern might be the bully in the neighboring block. She doesn't need to be told about gang tactics or rape statistics at a meeting for adults.

- skill focused. You'll want your child to come away feeling skilled rather than informed. A child is empowered only when he knows what to do and has had successful practice in the technique being taught.

- defense oriented. Ask the teacher of the course about his philosophy. Are the techniques being taught as defensive measures, or does the teacher desire to create little warriors?

Check Out the Videos Scout your local video rental store for titles that teach self-defense to children. Some of the videos are factual how-to approaches for *verbally* dealing with would-be molesters and abusers; others are stories that portray appropriate behavior on the part of children facing peer bullies or adult enemies. (Most of the latter are video versions of TV specials made for after-school viewers.) Avoid the Hollywood approach to self-defense, such as the *Home Alone* movies, when attempting to teach your child skills. Such portrayals may be fun, but they are unrealistic in preparing your child for actual emergencies.

Karate and Tae Kwon Do?

If you are considering a self-defense course for your child, be sure to ask the instructor about any religious overtones of a course. Most Eastern defense techniques are rooted in a philosophy of life that is distinct to the technique. An instructor of a course may see that philosophy *as* a religion and inadvertently or consciously teach it as such. You should be aware of that possibility.

When taught as a skills course without religious overtones, such an organized systematic approach to self-defense can give a child a great deal of courage and confidence, especially when facing peer bullies.

"Run and Holler"

Perhaps the simplest self-defense mechanism you can teach your young child is to "run and holler." If your child suspects that he is being routinely and systematically watched or followed, or if he is approached with an intent that seems malicious or an offer that seems too good to be true, he should run away as fast as possible and holler as he goes, "Stranger, stranger, stranger!" He should run toward a group of people or to a place where people will be, such as a store.

16 ° "I Am Your Defender"

Assure your child repeatedly that you will always be his number one friend, number one protector, and number one fan.

It does not mean, of course, that you will cover for her willful choices that bring harm to someone's property or person, make excuses for her bad behavior, or lie on her behalf.

A Proper Defense   It does mean that

- you will defend him against those who try to harm him. In some cases, you will help your child defend himself. In other cases, you will go to court on his behalf, confront abusers, or stand up for his rights as an innocent human being.

- you will not allow her to stay in abusive situations or force her to associate with those who abuse her. A child should know that if she is abused, you will take her side and put distance between her and her abuser.

- you will seek his best always. The best for your child may include difficult discipline and even punishment, but let your child know that your intent always is that he grow up to be a kind, honest, truthful, loving, and generous teenager and adult. In punishing your child now, you are actually defending him against greater punishment later!

Child-to-Child Combat   Children do fight. Verbal quarrels, "me first" jostling, and fights over territory and rights are a normal part of growing up. You can't vaccinate your child against the possibility of a black eye. Neither should you step in to rescue your child to the point that she consistently regards you as her bail provider.

If you find your child in a fight, intervene and separate him from the fray. Get to the bottom of the disagreement in a calm manner. If that isn't possible, leave the scene with your child.

As a parent, you have the right to set a standard within your home that lets your child know that

- both parties will be punished in a fight, no matter who starts it. Make it clear to your child that fighting is an inappropriate way to resolve problems. (This might include verbal fighting in which voices are raised, insults are hurled, doors are slammed, and so forth.) Thus, the child who fights on the playground may be spared punishment on site, but she is subject to punishment once at home.

- both parties will be required to face each other in a calm discussion about the problem.

- both parties will be required to apologize to each other for disturbing the peace of your home.

Watch for patterns in your child's fighting. If he always seems to be defending the same cause or giving vent to the same irritations, deal with him about that issue.

If your child's fights always seem to involve the same person, talk to the other child's parent about the rules you have established about fighting in your home, and suggest that both parents meet with the children to settle their feud in a rational sit-down-and-discuss-it manner. If the other parent is unwilling to settle grievances between the children in this manner, help your child find a new friend.

17 ☾ The Right Gear

Outer Gear Sometimes providing the right equipment or safety gear is the best thing you can do to help a child feel secure. Here are some examples:

- Training wheels for the bicycle

- Water wings for the swimming pool

- A life jacket for the boat

- A compass and a map for the hike

- A mosquito tent or can of insect repellant for the campout

- A tire pump for the bicycle

The right gear might be a red dot on a child's bedroom window (as a signal to emergency crews that a child lives in that room), an identification card to put in a wallet, or a medical bracelet if your child is diabetic.

The right gear might have to do not with personal safety but with the safety of property or the ability to access a place or person:

- A pair of boots to cover the new shoes

- A stamp on the back of the hand that allows reentry

- An umbrella of his own to carry in the rain

- A combination lock for the bicycle

Inner Gear The right gear for a particular situation might be training or information, as opposed to something tangible. For example, the right gear might be

- lessons. A child going to her first dance will feel a lot more secure if Mom or Dad has already taught her several dance steps or has provided her with a dance class.

- experience. A child will always feel more secure going to a place or trying an activity the second time.

- practice. A child will always feel more secure doing something that he has practiced repeatedly without an audience.

Both outer gear and inner gear are tools that help your child feel courage in a situation. Provide all you can!

18 ‘ "You Can Do It!"

Your child will feel more secure in a situation if *you* are secure with her being in that situation.

Parental Fears If you are nervous about your child going into the deep-water swimming pool, he'll be more apprehensive about it.

If you are uptight about how your child will be accepted at the party, she'll be more uptight about going.

If you are cotton mouthed at the thought of your child being up on the platform in front of everyone, he'll be much more prone to stage fright.

If you are wringing your hands at the idea of your child going up in an airplane, she's likely to be afraid of flying even before the plane takes off.

Parental Confidence Let your child know that you have confidence that he has what it takes to survive the challenge, to make it through the crisis, and to emerge from a situation healthy, whole, and stronger than ever.

Even before you drop your child off at school for the first day, tell her, "I know you have what it takes to do this. It takes a lot of courage, but you *have* a lot of courage."

As you drive your child to his first piano recital, say to him, "Do your best. Have fun. I know you've practiced hard. I know you know your pieces. And I believe you're going to come through this with flying colors."

Parental Don'ts and Do's Don't tell your child she is going to take first prize. Do tell your child that you'll be there as her number one fan.

Don't tell your child that he can't possibly make mistakes. Do tell your child that you are rooting for him and you believe in his abilities.

Don't offer your child a reward for success. Do tell your child that you love her—and that you will love her before, during, and after the event with an equal amount of love.

Don't put down other children or other teams. Do build up your child as being the most special player on the field in your eyes.

Be your child's biggest fan, most encouraging cheerleader, and staunchest ally. He'll feel a lot more courage as he faces the new challenge or the big moment.

19 ᶜ What If I Fall?

Because the fear of falling is so basic to the human psyche, there is probably very little you can do rationally to convince your child that he will not fall or cannot fall.

On the other hand, you can do a great deal to assure your child that she will survive a fall or that she will not fall without your notice and care.

Touch with a Steady Hand Be there to hold your child's hand or to steady his body as he has new experiences with balance—whether taking first steps, walking on the edge of a curb, putting on skates, or riding a bicycle for the first time.

Move Up Gradually If your child is afraid of heights, help her move up gradually. Perhaps she can begin walking on a curb before she tries walking close to the edge of a two-foot platform.

Fall with Her Jump into the pool with your child. Ride the Ferris wheel or the roller coaster with her so that she can see how you react to the experience of falling. If you are playing a game in which falling is part of the process (such as Ring Around the Rosy), fall along with your child.

Don't Force the Issue Don't *insist* that your child jump from high places. If your child is fearful of getting too close to the edge of an overhang, balcony, or ledge, let him stand back and view the world from a more remote stance. He'll come closer when he is comfortable and feels safe. Never make fun of your child for being afraid of falling.

Teach Your Child How to Fall This how-to is especially important in situations and games in which falling is inevitable and even desirable— such as tag football, ice skating, skiing, or sliding into second base. Show your child how to tumble and roll, how to jump clear of a bicycle, how to skid on her side to a halt. Teach your child how to walk on ice and how to relax her body if she begins to fall.

Teach Your Child How to Get Up After a fall, the best thing a person can do is to stay still a few moments. Take a couple of deep breaths. Untangle yourself slowly from any equipment involved (to avoid further damage to the body or to clothing and gear), and take stock of your injuries. Apply direct pressure to any bleeding. Get up slowly to lessen the possibility of fainting. Again, *show* your child the process; don't just describe it.

Have Fun on a Trampoline   Trampolines
are made for falling as much as for jumping. Let
your child learn various trampoline jumps and falls
under the supervision of a qualified teacher. He
may even come to see falling as fun!

**Explain the Difference Between Falling
and Leaping**   Teach your child the difference
between falling and willfully leaping. Anybody can
fall, and everybody does. Choosing to jump, however, is an act of the will. A child should be taught
never to jump into something that he hasn't experienced and tested fully at ground level first. Surfaces are rarely as soft, or water holes as deep, as
they may seem from a high vantage point. Hidden
obstacles or nearby hard surfaces can turn a play-
ful leap into a bloody or paralyzing accident.

On the other hand, an accidental slip, slide, or
tumble is not a fault. It should never be associated
with a label such as "clumsy," "uncoordinated," or
"silly." A fall is an accident, and it is normal. However, falls are to be avoided. Help your child learn
lessons from his spills to lessen the incidences and
results of future falls.

20 ❝ What If I Get Lost?

This question is usually asked when a child is facing a new environment: a school, a church, a playground, a forest, or a campground.

Sometimes the question is implied and not asked directly. For example, a child may exhibit clinging behaviors or a reluctance to say "goodbye." The child at that point is really thinking, *What if you get lost and can't find your way back to me? What if I'm stuck here forever without you?*

The solution to both situations is the same. Explore an area together.

A New School or Church Walk the halls with your child. Explore different turns. Point out certain landmarks that are unlikely to change and that your child can see even if the hallways are filled with people. Show your child where you will be in relationship to where he will be. Walk the path that connects the two of you. Your child will feel much more secure in knowing that he can get to you in an emergency, and that you know how to get to him.

The best time to explore an area is *prior* to an event in which you will be in separate places. You may want to visit a school several times during the summer months so that your child is thoroughly familiar with the buildings.

In the Wilderness or the Mall   Teach your child in advance what to do if you become separated—whether in the forest or the department store. The best thing your child can do is to *stop moving*. The more she continues to walk or run, the more likely she will be moving away from you or others who are looking for her. You might even suggest that she sit down.

If your child sits down in a department store, chances are that a clerk is going to ask her what she is doing. When that happens, advise your child to say, "I'm lost. Will you please call my mother or father?" Teach your child to give the clerk or security officer *your* name. Make sure your child knows your first and last names. Teach your child never to leave the store or area with anyone; tell her to follow a person with a badge or name tag only into an area in which she can see that other people are present.

The second thing your child can do is to *listen hard* for the sound of your voice or of the group he was with. A lost child tends to cry or to whimper, and the sound of his voice can blot out the sound of others. If a child hears a voice, he should call your name in the direction of the voice he heard.

Let Me Find You Assure your child that you will miss her presence about the same time she realizes she is lost, and that you will do your utmost to find her. Say, "If we get separated, let me find you. The best way you can do that is to stay put. I can see farther than you can see. I'll probably see you before you see me."

Lost and Found Before you set foot in a large area—such as an amusement park—have a backup plan. Tell your child where to go if you get separated and don't connect by a certain time. (Give yourselves a few minutes to be late.) Usually, that backup place can be the main entrance or the lost and found office of the park, mall, or building. Again, insist that your child not leave the area.

21 ᶜ What If You Aren't There on Time?

Short-Circuit Panic   Children tend to panic —or seek out mischief—if Mom or Dad doesn't show up at the appointed time. Help your child cope with your occasional tardiness.

Give your child a watch and teach him how to tell time   Sometimes minutes seem like hours to a child. A watch can help him see just how late you really are or aren't!

Set a grace period   Predetermine an amount of time that your child should wait patiently before concluding that you aren't coming. A grace period of ten or fifteen minutes will help you in times when the traffic lights just don't go your way.

Establish where your child should wait for you   If you don't want your child sitting on the bench at the bus stop or standing alone outside in the dark, give her specific instructions about where she should wait for you.

Suggest waiting activities   Teach your child to make the most of five- and ten-minute time periods —to read, make a list of homework that needs to be done, start an essay or story, or work a few math problems. He can turn a waiting period into a productive time. The minutes will go faster for him, and he'll have less opportunity to be concerned about your absence.

Have a backup plan Make sure that your child always has money for at least two phone calls, and that she knows numbers (by memory) to call should you fail to show up. Designate the persons to call. Make sure that both of you agree about what course of action she should take and what she should not do.

If your child must deviate from your agreed-upon backup plan for any reason (for example, because your spouse intervenes), he should be instructed to call and leave a message for you at his earliest convenience.

Develop a Habit of Promptness

Make tardiness the exception, not the rule. Your child should be able to count on your presence and on your arriving at a prescheduled time. The child who never knows when a parent might show up is a child who is likely to feel insecure, and who also will soon look for alternative activities to fill the spare time she comes to count on.

22 ‘ What If They Laugh at Me and Call Me Names?

Every child is laughed at or called a name at some point by some group, in some situation, or for some reason.

Helpful Explanations If your child is old enough to understand these reasons, share with your child that

- people sometimes laugh at others because they feel insecure. They try to put down others to build themselves up.

- people sometimes laugh at others because they are misinformed. Most laughter or name-calling that is about a person's race, learning disabilities, religion, or cultural differences is rooted in bigotry—a case of being misinformed about the value of all human beings.

- people sometimes laugh at others because they are actually trying to get to know that person. Name-calling can be a type of teasing to see what a person is like, find out how she will respond, and simply get her attention.

Helpful Advice These reasons may give some comfort to your older child, but the real help will be the advice about what to do. Say, "Laugh, too! Call yourself an even bigger and more hilarious name!"

If they are laughing at your appearance, say, "You should have seen how hard *I* laughed this morning when I looked in the mirror!" If they are calling you a nerd, let them know that you prefer to be called "the chief captain of the nerdiest division of Nincompoops Anonymous, subsection four, in the order of Nerds United International!"

It's very difficult for a person to make fun of someone who is willing to laugh at himself or have fun making fun! Such a person is actually very attractive, the kind of person most people want as a friend, not an object of ridicule.

On the other hand, the person who gets angry or who responds with name-calling taunts of her own is a person who is eager to pick a fight or who sets herself up to be picked on even more.

The Younger Child A child under the age of five is not likely to have the verbal skills to come up with spur-of-the-moment comebacks. Suggest to your young child that he smile, walk away, and find someone else to play with.

23 ' What If They Won't Let Me Play?

Every child at some point will be rejected by his peers—for at least a few minutes.

No child feels secure in the face of rejection.

Offer Tips About Play Here are tips for helping your child cope with those times.

Look for someone who doesn't have anyone to play with and play with him A child can nearly always find someone who is as alone as she is. She can seek out that person and befriend him. He is likely to be a better friend in the long run than those who reject your child.

Don't try to force your way into a group at play If some kids don't want your child to play with them at this time, he shouldn't force the issue. Reinforce in him the idea that membership in a play group tends to shift frequently. Just as your child feels closer to some children than to others, and his best friend may have changed several times in the past year, so play groups can shift from recess to recess. If the kids say, "Go away and leave us alone," the best response for your child to make is, "OK, I'll check you later!"

Play by yourself and have a good time Instill in your child the idea that it's OK to play alone, and that she can have fun playing by herself. In fact, she might even have so much fun that others will want to join her at play.

Watch Your Child at Play Periodically observe your child. Is he a good playmate? Does she share? Does he know how to play by the rules? Does she play fair? Is he hurtful (verbally or physically)? Is she cooperative or competitive? Does he insist on having his own way?

For your child to be accepted by a group, she must be a good playmate. Help your child develop the skills necessary for play with others. The best way to do this is to play with your child. Get down on the floor and engage in her activities, play with her toys, and make up stories that give roles for both of you to enact. Show her

- how to talk and how to listen.

- how to come up with ideas and how to let others come up with ideas.

- how to role-play and make up scenarios.

- how to help others.

The child who is willing to share his things, share leadership, and help others succeed will always be wanted as a playmate.

24 ꞏ What If I Have to Go to the Bathroom?

Every child seems to have a fear that she will have to relieve herself and either nobody will pay attention to her need or no facility will be available. Assure your child that you will do the utmost to heed her pleas for a rest room.

On Trips Plan to make periodic stops. Insist that your child try even if he doesn't feel an urgency at that time.

Some children wonder if rest room facilities are available on planes, trains, long-distance buses, and ships. Assure your child that a rest room will be available for his use.

Asking to Be Excused Teach your child to tell you of her need quietly, calmly, and privately. Also explain to your child in advance of her attending a party, meeting, special event, or outing that if she needs to relieve herself, she should quietly and privately express her need to the leader of the group.

Proper Terminology You may have euphemisms for various bodily functions within your family, but make sure that your child knows fairly generic phrases to express his need in public. It is always proper for him to say, "I would like to go the rest room, please. Can you tell me where it is?" (Or if your child is in a private home, he can ask, "Can you tell me where the bathroom is?")

At School Encourage your child to use the first few minutes of the recess periods or lunch break for a trip to the rest room. The child who makes the rest room her first stop on the way out to the playground or cafeteria will not get caught by a return-to-class bell that rings before she has taken care of her personal need.

Occasionally, a group of children in a school will block access to a rest room or claim it as their private turf. If that happens, and your child feels he can't complain to his teacher, speak up on your child's behalf. Rest room facilities in schools should be safe, clean, and well monitored. When you pick up your child at school, stop periodically to check out the rest room facilities. They will tell you a great deal about what is happening in your child's school as a whole.

Good Hygiene Insist that your child use paper seat covers whenever they are available (and to make her own from toilet tissue when they aren't provided) and that she wash her hands after using a toilet. Part of feeling secure is knowing that she isn't exposing herself to potential illness.

25 ❝ What If Someone Tries to Hurt Me?

Children frequently feel insecure in the presence of strangers, especially those who are bigger than they are. Children also express fear in the presence of people who have hurt them in the past.

If your child expresses a sudden repulsion or fear or has a fit of crying for no apparent reason, stop and look around. Who do you see? Is there someone your child doesn't want to see or be around? Question why, and if your child is old enough to answer your questions, explore the reason for the child's aversion in private.

Meeting Strangers Teach your child to extend a hand and say, "Hello," when she is introduced to someone she doesn't know. That's a positive move on your child's part and also a protection for the child who doesn't enjoy being kissed, held, or otherwise fawned over. Shaking hands is an appropriate move even for your child's peers, whether boy or girl.

A person's response to your child's outstretched hand might tell you and your child a great deal about the person. If the person rebuffs the handshake or uses it as an opportunity to cause pain, your child may need to avoid the person after the introduction is over.

What's Private Is Private Teach your child that certain parts of his body are private and no adult should touch them or fondle them. If an older child or adult tries, your child should firmly and immediately say, "No!" run away as quickly as possible to a group of people or an adult in whom he can confide, and tell the presiding adult what has happened. Assure your child that in no way has he done anything wrong, but that the other person *has* done something wrong and should be punished, and that you will do your utmost to see that justice prevails and this personal violation never happens again.

Discipline vs. Abuse Let your child know when you give permission to other adults to exact discipline or mete out punishment—whether it's a spanking, sending a child to her room, or denying certain privileges. Talk to other adults or teens with whom you might leave your child about what they may and may not do to and with your child. Express yourself clearly and directly to grandparents, aunts and uncles, older cousins and siblings, and baby-sitters and nannies.

If the boundaries you have established are breached, stand up for your child, and insist that your wishes as a parent be followed. If a second breach occurs, remove your child from the person's care, or make certain that you are always present with your child. (In cases of sexual abuse, don't even allow a second chance!)

Peer Bullies   If your child is threatened by a peer bully, he should walk away as quickly as possible and avoid confrontation. Bullies draw their power from an ability to threaten and get away with it. They are usually children who are bullied at home by an older sibling or who are experiencing abuse of some kind. Bullies nearly always try to pick a fight by first engaging in verbal taunts or name-calling.

Help your child make friends, and encourage him to use the buddy system when walking home from school. Bullies rarely pick on groups.

If the bully is an older child in your neighborhood, confront her yourself—but with friendship. See if there's a way you can help this child who finds a need to pick on younger, weaker children. In befriending the bully, you are nearly always putting your child beyond her threats.

26 ⸠ What If There's a Bad Accident?

Your child has two main lines of offense in times of emergency. Teach him how to use both!

Find an Adult Your child's first recourse in an emergency should be to find an adult. If you are unavailable or are the injured party, tell your child to run to the nearest neighbor or, away from home, to look for a person who is wearing a badge or name tag. (In most cases, a person with a badge or name tag will have some type of authority.) If an emergency happens at school, your child should run immediately to find a teacher, and if no teacher is available, she should go directly to the principal's office.

Dial 911 Show even your young child how to use the telephone to make 911 calls in cases of fire, serious illness or injury, or crimes he might witness.

Your child should be trained

- to speak slowly and distinctly.
- to know and to give his complete name and address.

- to note and give as many details as possible about the crisis that is under way.

Even children as young as two years of age have been able to call 911 for help when their parents have fallen into comas, experienced seizures, or been injured.

If your area doesn't have a 911 service, teach your child how to call the operator by dialing 0, and to identify herself first and foremost as a child who has a problem. She should say as soon as the operator answers, "I am a child, and I have a problem." Then she should state the problem. The operator will ask her name and address, which she should be trained to give quickly, distinctly, and accurately.

In teaching your child how to use a 911 service, emphasize that this number is only for emergencies. It is not for play or for pranks.

27 ⸰ What If I Can't Think of Anything to Say?

The child who is reluctant to talk is often fearful of being reprimanded for what he says or is afraid of being laughed at for saying the wrong thing or speaking in a wrong way.

Fear Busters Here are several ways that you as a parent or a loving adult friend can help a child overcome these fears or keep them from developing.

Encourage your child to talk, but don't force him to talk Ask questions. Pause in your conversation to allow for your child's opinions and comments.

Require that your child answer questions that are related to her safety and health, or to the safety and health of a person for whom you are responsible. But respect your child's desire, at times, to remain silent.

Listen to your child It's easy to tune out a child who seems to be talking just for the sake of talking. An adult needs to realize that "just for the sake of talking" is a legitimate reason for a child to talk! That's the way he will learn the language, become comfortable expressing himself, and grow to see himself as being an acceptable and valuable conversationalist. Be patient. Let your child tell the whole story his way.

Play word games and sing songs   One of the easiest ways to help a child overcome a fear of using the language or of vocalizing is to play word games, such as tongue twisters, alphabet games, and I Spy. Tell jokes and ask riddles. Share puns. Sing songs together.

If your child needs speech therapy, provide it for her Children who are afraid to talk usually have been laughed at because they sounded funny owing to a speech impediment. Never laugh at the way your child speaks. Insist that your child's siblings follow suit.

Never correct your child's speech patterns in public If your child mispronounces a word, uses a word incorrectly, or uses poor grammar, wait until you get home or alone and teach him the proper usage. Speak with an uncritical tone of voice—perhaps even saying, "I want you to be able to talk to others anyplace at any time so they'll listen to your valuable ideas and not stumble over a pronunciation, vocabulary, or grammar error."

Encourage your child to read   Reading builds a child's vocabulary, familiarizes her with new and unusual ways in which words can be put together, and gives her information and ideas to talk about! Ask her to read aloud to you as you prepare a meal. You'll give her good practice in vocalizing correct speech patterns.

Overcoming Stage Fright Many children experience stage fright. Given a sea of faces, even those who know an entire speech, song, or poem in rehearsal may find all the words in their minds evaporating and leaving behind a feeling of raw panic. Forearm your child for those moments as best you can:

- Arrange for your child to rehearse in front of an audience. Try to set up the rehearsal on the stage where the performance will be given.

- Teach your child to visualize the first three or four words of his presentation on the toes of his shoes. That way, when panic strikes, he can look down for a moment and imagine his beginning phrase. (Even children who aren't yet readers can associate their toes with words.)

- Let your child take a copy of what she is supposed to say in her pocket. For many children, this is a real confidence builder. Even though she may never need to resort to the paper, she knows that she can in a dire emergency.

No Ideas   Sometimes a child will simply feel as if he doesn't know what to say. In those times, encourage him to listen intently. He may not need to say anything. The best response may be for him to ask a question or to continue to listen intently. The more your child focuses on what the other person is saying, the more he'll have an idea or opinion to voice.

28 ' What If I Forget?

Many a child has exclaimed woefully, "My mind went blank!" An unsettling fear quickly settles in when a person—adult or child—is suddenly unable to recall something that she feels she should know or should remember.

Sharpen Up! Here are five tips for helping your child develop a good memory and avoid insecure moments.

First, assure your child that everybody forgets something at some time The best computers in the world occasionally have system errors or software glitches. The brain experiences the same lapses. If your child draws a blank, one way to overcome the feeling of panic is to admit that he has forgotten. He might respond, "I can't think of it right now, but I'm sure I'll remember it eventually."

Second, help your child learn something to the point that she can recall it A person generally needs to hear something or repeat something seven times before she has learned it to the point of committing it to memory. Of course, a child doesn't need to read a book seven times before grasping its meaning. But she probably needs to say "six times two equals twelve" or write out a spelling word correctly that many times. If you are sending your child to the store for "milk, eggs, and honey," ask her to repeat "milk, eggs, and honey" to herself as she goes—at least seven times.

Your child also needs to repeat certain behaviors again and again to make them habitual, which means that they are embedded in memory to the point of being automatic responses. If your child has a habit of forgetting his sweater, for example, give him a sweater to carry around the house. Each time he moves from one room to the next, he must remember to take his sweater with him. Make remembering a game. You'll still be creating a good new habit to replace a bad one.

Third, help your child encounter information in more than one sensory mode　For example, if you show your child a list of things to bring home from the store, ask her to read the list aloud so she hears it as well as sees it. If you tell your child to close the refrigerator door tightly after each time she opens it, write a note and put it on the fridge door, too. Seeing and hearing are two different sensory modes. The more sensory modes a child associates with information, the easier it is for her to recall the information later.

Fourth, teach your child how to use acronyms or to sort information in alphabetical or numerical order for easier recall　"Every good boy does fine" is a way to learn the names of the E-G-B-D-F lines on a music staff. "Gotcha three" is a way to remember to "get out the chicken at three o'clock" so it can be defrosted in time for dinner.

Fifth, give your child permission to ask again   If he forgets, he should ask for a repeat of the information. Here's a simple rule of thumb: "forgetting is OK; forgetting and acting as if you remember aren't."

29 ❝ What If I Wet My Pants?

Averting the Crisis Few things are as embarrassing to a child as his peers discovering that he has wet his pants or wet a bed.

Always heed your child's requests to use a rest room Don't say, "Just hold it." That may not be possible. Instead, say to her, "I'll find a place as quickly as possible."

Encourage your child to drink fluids on a steady, regular basis throughout the day Children who take in fluids on a steady, even basis—as opposed to drinking three glasses of water at a time because they haven't had anything to drink for several hours—seem to experience fewer bladder crises. (They also tend to be healthier.)

Put an end to your child's fluid intake a couple of hours before bedtime You may have to keep a close eye on your child for a few days to make this a new habit.

If your child has difficulty with bed-wetting, try getting her up at least once in the night Perhaps before you go to bed (assuming your child has already been asleep for a couple of hours), you can try this idea.

If a bed-wetting problem is chronic and persistent, consult a physician The doctor may refer you to a counselor. Some children have bed-wetting problems that are related to trauma in their lives. Others tend to sleep so deeply that their bodily needs don't awaken them. Help is available in both cases.

Coping with the Crisis You may want to keep a dry set of clothes for your child in your car. A change of clothes not only can help your child in a wet-pants crisis but will come in handy should he get caught in the rain or fall into a puddle.

If your child wets the bed while at another person's house, let her know in advance that she should tell an adult as soon as she realizes what has happened. There's no reason for your child to remain in a wet bed. The longer she does so, the more miserable and self-recriminating she'll be, and the greater the likelihood that others beyond the adult and the child will realize what has happened.

Assure your child that everybody has had this difficulty at some point in life.

Never laugh at your child for wet pants or a wet bed, make fun of him in front of others, or punish him for this behavior. Insist that your other children refrain from laughing. Don't recount or retell the incident. Let the behavior slide into the past without fanfare or notice.

30 ' What If You Die?

Children nearly always come to this question at some point in their growing-up years. Those with parents who travel a great deal may suddenly feel insecure about a parent who is leaving on a flight (perhaps after just seeing a plane crash report on television), or those who feel the pain of a grandparent's death or who witness what happens as the result of death in a friend's family may have an overwhelming sadness about the possibility of a parent's death.

What Can You Say? Several responses are appropriate no matter what the situation that causes your child to ask the question.

Let your child know that you have made provisions for him to be taken care of should you die A child's primary concern is with his well-being. "Who will take care of me if you aren't here?" may be the question that is really being asked. Make sure your child knows with whom he would go to live. If you haven't made a legally binding arrangement with a family member, godparent, or friend, see your attorney and do so. Your child will be reassured further if that person will say to him, "If any-thing ever happens to your mom and dad and they are unable to care for you—which I pray won't hap-pen—I'm here for you."

Assure your child that you want to live as long as you possibly can—for your child's sake and for your own Tell her that you are going to do your utmost to live a safe and healthful life. Express to her your will to live.

Speak to your child realistically about death, grief, and going on with life Following the death of a pet, you may want to bring up these matters. Talk with your child about the fact that every living thing dies—whether it is a human being, a pet, or a plant. The important thing is to live life to the full-est and then to be prepared to die. Assure your child that you have made peace with God and you are looking forward to living in heaven someday—in fact, you are looking forward to spending all eternity with God and with your child. Talk about the joy of heaven and your hope of an eternity that is without sickness, pain, sorrow, lack, loss, or death. Talk about heaven in real terms; help your child visualize it as a wonderful, real place. Talk about people from your past who are in heaven and about the joy you feel at the thought of seeing them again. Give your child the hope of heaven.

Let your child know that it's OK to cry and to feel sadness after a death. Grief is a normal part of living, and it sometimes includes anger, tears, and a great sense of pain and loss. These feelings are normal. The day comes, however, when life must be rejoined.

Invite your child to pray with you about her safety and health Before you leave on a trip, have a prayer with your child for your safety and well-being in travel and for her safety and well-being at home.

Assure your child always that God has a plan for his life, which includes providing for him the things and the people he needs Help your child memorize Psalm 10:14: "You [God] are the helper of the fatherless." Assure your child that when parents die or when parents fail, children are not without a heavenly Father who loves them and cares for them.

31 ‘ Will They Like Me?

One of the most helpful things you can teach your child is the twofold truth that not everybody likes everybody else, but there's somebody who will like every person.

People Like . . . You can enhance the possibility that your child will be among the "liked." Teach your child some basics about people.

People like other people who help them and speak well of them Teach your child how to be a fan of another person without worshiping the person or fawning over her. A child can learn to be generous in compliments and positive affirmation: "Way to go!"; "You played a great game today!"; "You got an *A?* Fantastic!" Teach your child that his approval of someone else doesn't diminish his approval rating. If anything, it raises his approval rating in the eyes of every person who receives such a compliment or overhears him giving one.

People like people who show basic good manners That means being kind and considerate and sharing what they have. Is there someone with whom your child can share half her candy bar? Does your child say "please" and "thank you" even to peers? Does your child let others take a turn, go first, or tag along? If not, teach your child that good manners and general kindness go a long way in being liked.

People like people who take the time to get to know them   That includes asking questions about them, listening to them, and spending time with them. It's easy to dismiss a person as unlikable or to draw a conclusion that you aren't liked after just a few minutes in someone's presence. Perhaps he's having a bad day. Perhaps she is shy or is trying too hard. Perhaps he is reacting to an incident that has just happened and not to your child at all!

Encourage your child to cut people slack and to give himself and others a chance for a relationship to grow and develop naturally over time.

Finding Someone to Befriend   The best way to gain a friend is to be a friend. If your child is rejected by another child or group of children, encourage your child to seek out someone who needs a friend. Encourage your child always to

- keep the secrets of her friend (as long as they are not secrets directly related to health, safety, or abuse issues).

- speak well of his friend. Criticism kills friendship—whether direct or indirect.

- avoid gossip.

- take the time to spend time. Friendships take time. A friend is needed most in a crisis. If your child's friend is going through a rough period, allow your child the freedom to spend time with that friend.

Tolerating the Intolerable Teach your child that she can learn to tolerate people she dislikes or people who seem to dislike her. She can learn to tolerate their presence and to be considerate around them.

What does this have to do with your child being liked? Others will observe how your child treats someone who may be mean or indifferent to him. If your child continues to be friendly and even-tempered toward that person, the observer is likely to conclude, "That's the kind of person I want as *my* friend."

32 (What If I Can't Do It By Myself?

Children sometimes feel insecure about their inability to do something that others seem to think they can do.

Step at a Time   Help your child move into a new skill or experience with graduated steps.

Your child may not be able to spell all two hundred words on the standardized spelling test the first time he hears them. But he can probably learn how to spell twenty new words a week for the next ten weeks.

Your child may not be able to ride a bike by herself the first time she gets on one, but with a little stabilizing guidance from you, she can probably learn to ride a bike within a couple of days.

Basic Skills   Your child needs to learn certain skills essential to his general sense of self-esteem:

- Dressing himself, including tying his shoes and buttoning his shirt

- Brushing his teeth and taking a bath

- Going to the bathroom by himself

As your child gets a little older, he should know how to cook a simple meal, do a load of laundry, and clean his room.

Project Independence   Here are more tips for helping your child gain independence.

Always hold out the hope of independent behavior Say to your child, "You may not be able to do this by yourself right now, but someday you will be able. I'll help you until you can do it by yourself." Just because your child can't do something now doesn't mean she will never be able to do it.

Always assure your child that your feelings about him won't change with independence Don't say, "I'm going to miss doing this for you," or "I'm going to hate the day when you no longer need me." Instead, say, "I want to help you grow up to be independent of my hands and feet but never totally separated from my heart."

Show your child how to read instructions and follow them Let the instructions be your first resort to fixing something, making something, or resolving a problem. The same goes for getting information you need. If your child can't do something on her own because she lacks information, teach her where and how to ask for the facts, procedures, or protocol she needs to know.

Give your child an opportunity to practice alone Don't look over his shoulder at every step. Let him try a skill in private.

Let your child know that it's perfectly acceptable to ask for help   There's no crime in asking another person for information or assistance. The person may choose not to give what is asked for, but that's a separate issue. It's not a sign of weakness or a fault to ask for help.

Teach your child to focus on what she can do, not on what she can't do   If your child can do only part of a task, permit her to do that part. Your child may not be able to fold and put away all the clothes, but she can probably fold the washcloths.

Tell your child that you expect him to do his best and try his hardest but you don't expect perfection   Nobody is perfect or can do everything perfectly all the time.

33 ‘ What If I Get Sick?

Children rarely ask this question unless they are already feeling sick or they have become ill in the past away from home.

Chicken Soup Needed Here? Reassure your child that if he isn't feeling well, you will provide a place and means for him to recover as best you can.

- Check for visible signs of illness—a change in countenance, listless behavior, a fever.

- Ask your child to describe her symptoms and their onset. If the situation seems severe enough for you to miss work or arrange for sick-child care, do so. Don't let your child go to school or be around other children if she is ill.

- Insist that if your child is sick enough to stay home, he must go to bed and stay there most of the day—no TV watching, no playing games, no all-day snacking, no friends coming over. A child who is truly ill will want to sleep, won't feel much like talking or play-

ing, and will desire to consume mostly liq-
uids.

• If your child suddenly improves a great deal
the minute you've agreed to stay at home
with her or to let her skip school, realize
you've been conned, and insist that your
child dress and go to school—even if she
misses half a day.

Some children use this fear to talk their way into
staying home from school, camp, or another event
—or to manipulate Mom or Dad into spending
time with them. If you suspect you are being
manipulated, talk about the root fear with your
child. What does he fear about school or camp?
Appraise the time you spend with your child. Are
you spending enough time with him?

A Bad Experience   If your child has been ill
in the past at a party or at school, she may have
insecurity that she will become ill again, especially
if she has a nervous stomach. Assure your child
that if she feels the need to see the school nurse or
to arrange to come home from a party, she need
only ask and you will be there as quickly as possible to pick her up. If your child is feeling nauseous,
she can always ask to be excused to go to the rest
room or to go outside for some fresh air.

34 ❝ Will You Ever Leave Me?

Reassure Regularly Assure your child as often as you need to that you will never run out on him. Explain some things to him, however—as soon as he is able to understand what you are saying.

To abandon is not the same as to leave Parents sometimes need to leave—to take business trips, to deal with emergencies, to find a job, to move in advance of the sale of a house or in case of marital separation or divorce. To leave is to go away with the intent of coming back or of being rejoined as a family. To abandon is to cease to care for, to provide for, or to love.

If you find yourself facing a family breakup, make it clear to your child that your leaving has nothing to do with your feelings for her, that she is not responsible for your leaving, and that you will not be abandoning her in terms of love, provision, or care.

Sometimes a person is unwillingly separated from those he loves An example would be illness, military service, or some type of calamity. Explain to your child that you intend and desire never to be separated accidentally from him.

Be sure your child knows that when you drop her off at a Sunday school class or a summer camp session you are not rejecting her, abandoning her, or ceasing to care for her If at all possible, set for your child a specific time when you anticipate that you will be together again. Say, "This is only for an hour," or "We'll be back to pick you up in exactly fourteen days." If your child is too young to tell time or read a calendar, talk to her in terms she does understand: "I'll be back to get you by the time you have played with all the toys on that shelf."

If your child clings to you in fear that you will never come back, try staying a few minutes with your child in the new environment Help him make a new friend and begin to play.

Return When You Say   You can alleviate the sense of insecurity associated with being left by making it a habit of returning for your child promptly. Greet your child with a positive message: "I came back for you just as I said I would, and I'm even five minutes early!"

Let your child know she can count on your word regarding time and place, and she'll feel much more confident that she can rely on your promise never to abandon her.

35 ‹ What If That Creature Hurts Me?

A child's fear of animals, insects, and reptiles very often stems from an early experience in which the child perceived that an animal larger than himself was threatening him or from an experience in which an adult reacted with fear-causing intensity to the presence of a creature near the child.

Stay Calm You can do a great deal to keep the latter fear from developing or to alleviate its power. If you see your child in a situation that you believe is dangerous, move quickly but calmly to her, and remove her from the presence of the animal or insect. Make few comments before, during, and after your maneuver. In other words, no screaming, no hysterics, no tears. Hold your child close as a means of expressing your relief that she is safe, and perhaps say to her, "Mommy just needed a big hug," or "Daddy wants to show you something over here."

  If there's an insect, reptile, rodent, or other creature that needs to be killed or removed from the area, do so out of sight of your young child's view (if at all possible).

Advance Education   Alert your child to the danger associated with certain animals, insects, and reptiles. You might go through a picture book with him and point out various living things with the question, "What would you do if you saw one of these in the garden?" or the statement, "If you see one of these, here is what you need to do."

If you have an infestation in your yard or house that could be dangerous to your child, capture one of the creatures, if possible, and show it to your child. Let him know that it is dangerous and that he should alert you quickly if he spots one.

The "Calm Escape"   Teach your child the value of a calm escape. Animals and insects tend to react to sudden movement with bared teeth, stingers, and strikes. Teach your child to back away slowly and calmly or to stand very still ("like a statue") and let the snake, animal, or insect move away of its own accord.

Graduated Experience   If your child has a fear of dogs, for example, perhaps the dog that was big to your child at the time he was frightened was actually an average-sized dog. The fear remains, however, to the point that even a small dog can send the child into a panic.

Help your child overcome this fear with a puppy of her own. Puppies are rarely frightening. As your child watches her puppy grow, she will learn about dog behavior and will come to feel that there is at least one dog about which she has no fear.

Petting Zoos Take your child to a petting zoo from time to time so that he can become familiar with some animals up close and personal. Take him horseback riding. Visit zoos and aquariums. Let your child see that animals are usually non-threatening; in fact, they rarely threaten human beings unless they are provoked, they are trained to attack, their turf is invaded, or they are surprised.

36 ' What If I Don't Like It?

Encourage your child to experiment with various aspects of his culture. A child's maturity and social acceptability seem directly related to his variety of experiences, most of which should be directly supervised or authorized by an adult.

Foods A child frequently registers a dislike for a certain food because she sees an adult rejecting it or treating it with suspicion. Assume that your child *will* like spinach. Give new foods to her with the approach, "Here's a great new flavor sensation." If your child rejects the food, don't assume that she will *never* like it. Try it again in a few weeks, months, or even years. Don't assume that her tastes will mirror your own. Your child may enjoy the very food you detest.

Encourage your child to experiment with herbs and spices as he grows older. Also encourage him to cook. Suggest that your child try at least a small bite of a new dish or food so he will *know* if he likes it or not.

Don't force your child to eat foods she doesn't like. Find a food in the same general category (with the same nutritional value) that your child does like and offer her that. Avoid sweets and heavily processed foods. They truly dull the taste buds.

Teach your child how to discard a bite of food politely (by spitting it into a napkin or excusing himself from the table for a moment).

Clothing Within the range of your budget and general good taste, allow your child to participate in the decision about what he will wear. Let him help pick out items at the time of purchase. Teach him to trust in his sense of style and ability to put together a "look" rather than to rely on designer labels. Emphasize quality construction (show your child how to determine if a garment is well made), washable materials, low-maintenance styles, and "mixability" of an item with other elements in the child's wardrobe. On a daily basis, let your older child put together his own look. As you dress a young child, explain why you are putting certain garments, colors, and fabrics together.

Your Child's Room Involve your child in decorating her room. Choose furniture and fabrics for comfort and easy maintenance. Let your child participate in the choice of colors and designs. Make the decorating of her room a mutual project. A child should always feel at home in her space— not as a visitor in a showroom.

Cultural Experiences Never assume that your child won't like a particular kind of exhibit or performance. Allow him to evaluate the experience of opera, a symphony concert, or a museum for himself. Children frequently express boredom with a cultural experience because they are over-exposed to it. Leave at intermission, or view only one wing of the gallery. Seek out performances aimed at children or ones based on classic stories with which children are familiar. Also seek out hands-on exhibits, museums, and performances in which your child is invited to participate in some way. Such experiences are nearly always positive.

37 ❝ What If I Break It or Ruin It?

Your child will feel insecure about breaking or ruining an object or item of clothing in direct proportion to the value that you place on the item.

Plan Ahead You can reduce a child's anxiety level about things in several ways.

Choose childproof items at the outset If you prefer ceramic dishes and breakable glassware to plastic dishes and glasses, choose patterns that will be easy and inexpensive to replace and that conform to a child's hands. Expect items to be broken from time to time!

Choose furniture that will stand up to a child's sticky fingers, spills, and bangs. Choose clothing that is flexible and sturdy and has minimal frills to snag. Whenever possible, choose the alternative that is washable—whether it's with crayons and paints, stuffed animals, clothing and upholstery fabrics, or window and floor coverings.

If you own valuable items, lock them away or put them well out of your child's reach until he gets older.

Set aside certain areas of your home for eating and playing   Keep food consumption confined to a kitchen or specified eating area. Encourage your child to play outdoors as much as possible. Teach her to wipe her feet or take off her muddy shoes before entering the house. Choose furniture and fabrics for an indoor play area that will stand up to a child's lack of coordination and tendency toward an occasional outburst of rambunctious rowdiness.

Expect your child to own up to accidental breakage or staining as quickly as possible   That way, you can make sure that all pieces are swept up (especially glass) or that the stain might be removed before it becomes permanent.

Teach your child what you consider to be the difference between accidental and willful destruction of property   The child who "accidentally" hits a ball through a neighbor's window while playing in an area where he has been told not to play is a child who should be subject to punishment. The child who knocks over a glass of milk while receiving a bowl of mashed potatoes is a child who has had an accident.

Teach your child the principle of retribution for the victim   Your child should help pay for damage incurred to another person's property (including your property or that of a sibling or friend). The amount contributed toward replacing the shattered glass or broken toy is likely to be prorated, of course, to the child's ability to pay. The amount should be significant enough, however, to get his attention and require his diligence, sacrifice, or extra work.

Your child should always be taught to apologize for acts of destruction. But an apology should accompany retribution, not be a substitute for it.

Recognize personally and teach your child that things are for now but people are forever Ultimately, every possession will be broken, damaged, or discarded. Very few things that exist today will be around a hundred years from now. On the other hand, relationships with people have the capacity to be eternal. Showing respect for another person's property is a way of showing respect for that person. And respect is a key ingredient necessary for long-standing relationships.

38 ⸱ What If I Have to Go to the Dentist, Doctor, or Hospital?

A child's insecurity about dentists, doctors, and hospitals nearly always boils down to two fears: fear of the unknown, and fear of pain. Help your child in these ways.

Insist Upon Honesty Never tell your child that something isn't going to hurt or isn't going to be uncomfortable if there's any chance at all that it might be! The better approach is to say, "This is going to sting, and it's going to sting to the count of ten. As soon as you feel the pain, start counting!"

Provide a Mental Escape Give your child something positive and pleasant to think about during certain procedures. Say, "While the dentist is drilling, imagine that you are in a mine and you are about to find a rich vein of gold. Make up a story in your head. When the dentist fills your tooth, think about how much you try to cram into your backpack when you spend the night at Grandma's."

Go with Your Child Don't send your child to the dentist's chair or the physician's examining room alone. Go along. Your presence will be of comfort to your child as long as you are calm and confident.

Be Informed Ask questions of the doctor in your child's presence. Have your doctor explain things to you in terms that your child can also understand. Don't have secrets from your child about a medical condition or a course of treatment. Encourage your child to ask questions, too, about how certain instruments work, what certain supplies are used for, and why the doctor does certain procedures or orders certain tests.

Visit in Advance If your child is facing hospitalization (perhaps for a tonsillectomy or other type of surgery), arrange for an advance visit to the hospital. See where your child will be staying or spending the night. Your child will feel much more secure going back to the hospital a second time.

If at all possible, describe for him various parts of the hospital and roles of key hospital personnel (nurses, doctors, aides, and so on). Tell him why the doctor will be wearing a "uniform" and a mask and gloves.

Stay the Night   One fear about going to a hospital is usually the fear of spending a night away from home in a strange place and bed. If possible, stay with your child in the hospital until she falls asleep. (Some hospitals allow parents to stay overnight in the rooms of young patients.) Don't tell your child that you'll be there when she awakens unless you are absolutely sure that you will be. Do tell your child that the nurse is available to help her at all times, and make sure that she meets the nurses who will help her. Show her, prior to your leaving the hospital, how to call for a nurse.

Don't Overreact   Don't respond to your child's appearance, news of your child's diagnosis, or the moment of separation from your child with expressions of fear, panic, or anxiety. Keep your tears and expressions of fear out of your child's view or hearing. He'll recover faster, do better, adapt more quickly to his surroundings, and feel more confident if he doesn't have to worry about *your* feelings and fears. As much as possible, be matter-of-fact about the work that doctors, dentists, nurses, and surgeons do.

Have Faith   Whatever the condition, prognosis, or circumstance, express to your child your belief and hope that she *will* get better and that she *will* live a long, joyful, and productive life. Believe that for your child always.

39 ❛ What If They Dare Me to Do Something Wrong?

Children are frequently caught off guard when friends dare them to do something they don't want to do or know they shouldn't do. The dare may be couched simply as an invitation. Either way, the child feels fear—at the proposed act or at the thought of punishment should he be caught in the act! You can help your child cope with these moments.

Forearm Your Child Explain to your child that his peers will sometimes want him to do things that aren't good or safe for him. Reinforce to him that it is *always* your desire that he see, experience, taste, or try things that are for his benefit. Tell him boldly and directly—on more than one occasion—that your greatest desire is to see him grow up to be a confident, healthy, generous, and courageous adult. Having courage and staying healthy sometimes mean saying no to friends who *don't* care what kind of teenager or adult your child becomes.

Give Your Child an Automatic "Out"

Let your child know that she can always say, "No, I'd rather not." She doesn't need to give excuses. Regardless of the names your child may be called or the teasing that might ensue, her decision is a good one, and she should stick by it with courage. Always applaud your child's refusal to go along with mischief or a dangerous activity as an act of courage.

You might also want to offer your child these responses to make: "Who do you think I am? I'm too smart for that!"; or "I have other plans." Again, he doesn't need to explain the plans. He can simply respond if asked, "They're *my* plans."

If your child finds herself in a place where she is uncomfortable, she should leave immediately and call you to pick her up. She can excuse herself to her friends by saying, "I just remembered that I need to be someplace else right now."

Encourage Your Child to Lead Rather Than to Follow

The best alternative to a dare or an unsafe invitation is a positive, fun, safe activity. Most children would rather *not* do things that they think might be harmful, painful, or punishable. Help your child think of creative ways to turn a friend's or group's attention away from the daring activity to the delightful activity. If, for example, a friend dares your child to see an X-rated video, your child might respond, "I think that would be boring. I'd rather go outside and play catch."

As you talk to your child about how to field a dare, teach him about the difference between being a leader and a follower. A good leader comes up with ideas that are good for everybody, and he is willing to express those ideas. Activities that are geared toward cooperative play, service to others, or learning (good information) are nearly always beneficial to every child in a group. List some of those activities with your child. Remind him how enjoyable those activities have been to him in the past and how good he feels after engaging in them.

40 (What If Someone Offers Me Drugs?

Many adults automatically assume that drug use is entirely the result of peer pressure. Peer pressure to participate is one aspect of drug use, but it is not the sole reason children choose to say yes to an experiment with or to ongoing use of chemicals. A major part of the appeal that drugs hold for children—even young children—is linked to these two reasons:

1. Drugs seem to be part of the adult domain. Therefore, a child perceives himself to be more of an adult if he uses chemicals.
2. Drugs offer an alternative to the way a person is presently feeling—either as an escape or as empowerment. A child who is feeling insecure or fearful is especially prone to experimentation as a means of feeling more confident.

Preemptive Measures A parent can address drug use in several preemptive ways.

Stop any chemical abuse If you are using chemicals, you are impotent in telling a child not to use them. A child will copy the behavior he sees much more readily than he will do what he is told. If you resort to chemicals to alleviate stress in your life or to be more sociable, your child will seek out chemicals for the same purposes.

Recognize, and convey to your child, that alcohol, tobacco, strong prescription medicines, and various types of pills are addictive Further, explain that anything that is addictive and causes physical harm is to be avoided. Medicines, on the other hand, generally help a person to recover from an ailment.

Give your child advance warning Give your child skills in how to deal with an offer of alcohol, pills, inhalants, or tobacco. "Just say no" is certainly a good beginning. Encourage your child to add a self-esteem statement to that line, such as, "I'm too smart to buy that argument," or "I know what this stuff can do to the brain, and I'm planning to use my brain for other things." Explain to your child that people who offer chemicals to him are not friends because they are not seeking his best and brightest health or future. Let your child know that she doesn't need to engage in an argument on the subject, but that she can just walk away from the offer.

As your child grows, talk to him about the scientific data linking various chemical substances to illness and death Provide facts to bolster his arguments against those who may continue to try to entice him with dares, pleas, or threats of alienation.

Intervention If you suspect that your child has experimented, or is experimenting, with chemicals, intervene immediately. Get help from professionals. Address underlying feelings of insecurity and estrangement that may be at the root of your child's desire to escape reality or be more a part of the group.

41 ☾ What If I Don't Know What to Do?

Adults aren't the only ones who sometimes find themselves at wit's end. Children, too, sometimes just don't know what to do, where to turn, or how to cope.

Perhaps the best advice can be summed up in three words: *ask for help*.

Wise Counselors Teach your child to seek out *wise* counselors, ones who will give him advice that is for his benefit, advice that lines up with your values, and advice that causes no harm to others. Your child also needs to seek out wise counselors who are *knowledgeable* in the area in which he needs help.

If the first person that your child seeks out isn't wise, doesn't have the knowledge, or refuses to help, your child should seek out a second person and perhaps a third or fourth until she gets the help she needs.

Assistance Only Your child should be taught the difference between getting assistance and having a person *do* the task or job for him. Children frequently ask for help in hopes that someone will do the job they detest, don't want to do, or are having trouble with. Help your child, but don't do the chore or homework for him.

The same holds for advice about what to do in relationships or in difficult circumstances. She should choose a counselor who will help her make the right decisions, not a person who will tell her what to do or make decisions for her.

Smart Assistance   Here are some situations in which your child can benefit greatly by asking for help if it's needed:

*   Directions: "If the directions aren't clear, or if you need directions on how to get to the place you want to go, ask! Don't wander around lost."

*   Procedures: "If you don't readily understand the instructions for putting something to-gether—whether it's a model airplane or a cookie recipe—ask for clarification! Don't end up with a disaster."

*   Skills: "If you don't know how to position ele-ments together or manipulate tools, ask!" If you are the teacher of a skill, make sure the child has an opportunity to rehearse in your presence. Don't show and leave. Let your child practice the skill at least once in your presence, and then leave so she can work on her own.

- Definitions: "If a person uses a word or phrase you don't understand, ask about the meaning. Don't pretend to know. If you can't ask the person, look up the word as soon as you can so you'll remember the context in which you heard it."

Modeled Behavior The wise parent or adult will model asking behaviors for children. The child who sees an adult asking for clarification, admitting what he doesn't know, and seeking help will be a child who learns faster and more than other children. The child who knows either what to do or how to get help is a secure child.

42 ꞉ What If It Won't Hold Me Up?

Children sometimes reflect insecurity and fear about the ability of mechanical objects, natural formations, and furniture to hold them up. This fear is closely related to the fear of falling. It might even be considered anticipatory fear of falling. It's an instinct that can serve your child well as long as it doesn't totally cripple his willingness to explore the world around him.

Testing for Strength Show your child how to put weighty objects on a device to test its ability to withstand her weight—including her putting partial weight on an object to test its sturdiness. Teach your child how to look for

- stress cracks.

- the strength of joints.

- the tightness of connections.

A rowboat with wide cracks isn't likely to hold your child up in the water; a rope ladder with frayed rope strands isn't likely to hold your child; a wall with crumbling stones isn't a safe place to walk.

If you live in an area where ponds and rivers freeze over in the winter, you must teach your child the signs of thin ice and what to do if ice begins to crack. A young child should understand that she is not to go out on ice without your permission.

Too Little Trust   Many Scouting, wilderness, and camping groups have "trust" exercises in which groups of children uphold a single child. Such an exercise may be helpful to your child if he struggles with having too little trust of objects that are otherwise strong enough.

Too Much Trust   The greater tendency of children is to assume that everything will hold them up. They usually aren't aware of their growth, their weight, or the ways of determining the stability of an object. Teach your child a simple rule of thumb: "don't trust it to hold you up unless you feel sure it would hold up Mom or Dad."

43 ❝ What If I Fail?

Failure looms as an issue for a child in direct proportion to the *consequences* the child perceives will occur if he fails.

Standards of Acceptability—Not Perfection Never set up a standard of perfection for your child. She won't reach it—to her dismay and your frustration. The problem with standards of perfection is that they are subject to individual interpretation, and the better the performance tends to be, the higher the standard of perfection moves!

Teach your child that you consider it to be very important to

- complete tasks once started. Insist that your child finish the tasks she starts. If she wants to sign up for trumpet lessons, make sure you have an agreement in advance about how much she must practice daily and how long she must take lessons. In most cases in life, it's better to be a completionist than a perfectionist.

- give a task his best effort. Insist that your child give any activity his best effort; otherwise, he'll never know how good he is or where his talents lie.

- do a task with joy. The child who grits her teeth at every task or finds no pleasure in accomplishing a goal is being asked to do too much or is requiring too much of herself. Encourage your child to have fun testing the limits of her skills.

- be willing to try again. Most failures can be reversed. They can be overcome with practice, new circumstances, or greater physical development. Never let your child assume that because he has failed once he can never succeed at the task in the future. The old adage, "If the horse throws you, get right back on it," is a good one for most circumstances.

- learn from failure. For a failure to be turned into a success, one must learn from the failure. What went wrong? Why? What can be done to correct that situation? Where is the weakness? How can it be overcome? Analyze a failure to the point of deciding what to change or fix, but don't dwell on a failure or play it over and over again.

Failing vs. Being a Failure Never let your child internalize a failure to the point that she thinks of herself as a failure. Tell her as often as you need to, "Failure is the result of what we do or don't do. Failures are not what we are!"

Never let your child transfer a failure at one task to another situation or circumstance. Just because your child fails a math test doesn't mean that he's going to fail a spelling test! Encourage him to see himself with both strengths and weaknesses. The strengths are to be built upon; the weaknesses are to be overcome.

Winning and Losing   Teach your child that life has numerous opportunities for winning and losing. No one wins all the time; no one loses all the time. The important thing is to be a generous winner and a gracious loser. Encourage your child to be kind to others when she wins and to congratulate the winner when she loses.

Never link approval of your child to what he wins. Winning is the result of competition, and correlating approval with winning sends a message to your child that he is being compared to other children when it comes to your love. Your child should be assured that you love him solely *because* he is your child, no matter what other children may do or not do.

44 ☾ What If I Don't Obey?

A child is more secure if he knows where the boundaries of behavior lie and what will happen should those boundaries be breached. In other words, a child wants discipline and guidance.

Let your child know in advance what he may—and may *not*—do in certain situations at certain times. Be clear about when a rule is always a rule and when it is a temporary rule governed by a situation. (For example, you may tell your child that it is time for her to be quiet when entering the church sanctuary. You certainly, however, don't mean for her not to sing hymns or respond when appropriate during the service. The better directive would be to tell your child, "No talking during the sermon.")

Define Good Behavior Don't tell your child simply to behave or to play nicely or not to run. Define good behavior and appropriate play activity. Be specific. Your child needs to hear concrete examples.

- Say, "Don't run into the street or down the sidewalk."

- Say, "Don't hit, pinch, or tickle the person next to you."

- Say, "Don't get into the cookie jar without permission."

Whenever possible, give your child boundaries he can see or experience, and also provide a positive alternative to misbehavior.

- Say, "I'm happy to give you my full attention when I'm off the phone, but I don't want to be interrupted while I'm talking to someone. If it's urgent, write me a note or give me a danger sign; otherwise, wait."

- Say, "You may play anywhere in the back yard or front yard, but you may not leave our yard."

- Say, "You may read your Bible or work your Bible puzzle book during the sermon, but you may not talk."

Define the Terms of Punishment Don't barter with your child, and don't let your child test *your* limits in exacting punishment. Expect your instructions to be obeyed the first time you give them, not the fifth time you plead for obedience. Hold firm to the rule that willful disobedience is subject to punishment.

Whatever terms of punishment you establish, make certain that

- your child knows the terms of punishment.

- you follow through. Don't make idle threats. Do what you have told your child you are going to do.

Then, and only then, can a child trust you to be true to your word *all* the time. Then, and only then, can a child feel secure that your boundaries are fixed and not subject to whim. If she suspects that your boundaries are based on whim, she'll do her best to manipulate you to change your mind. A tug-of-war ensues. And the sad result is that your child never fully knows where you stand, and she never fully knows where she stands. Such a child is insecure—always testing and struggling to discover what she can count on with certainty.

45 ꞌ What Are You Saying About Me Behind My Back?

It's No Joke   Children are just as prone to the ill effects of gossip as adults are. They feel insecure when they suspect that someone is talking about them behind their backs, making fun of them when they aren't watching, or enjoying a joke at their expense when they aren't present.

Always tell your child the truth (as you perceive it) about life and about him   Never lie to your child. Little white lies can turn into deceitful behavior and manipulation in your child. Blatant lies often translate into a distorted view of reality.

Always be forthright with your child   If you and your spouse make a decision about your child's health, safety, welfare, education, or relationships, let her know your decision. Don't leave her guessing. Provide as many details about the decision as you can, and answer her questions fully.

Never discuss your child's private fears or share his secrets with others   Earn the trust of your child by keeping his confidences.

Never require your child to keep family secrets that cover for the illegal, immoral, abusive, or addictive behavior of one family member A family is only as sick as the secrets it chooses to keep and the lies it chooses to tell to itself and to others.

Keep any critical or instructive comments you make to your child within your relationship Don't assume that because you have told your child a truth about herself you are now at liberty to share that truth with everyone else. Your criticism will hurt doubly if your child overhears a critical comment about herself being voiced to others. Be your child's fan and teacher, not her critic.

How can you assure your child that you will not spread gossip or unkind comments about him? By monitoring closely your behavior and your conversations about others. Your child will listen closely to hear what you say about others in their absence. If he hears you telling lies, spreading gossip, or revealing confidences of others, he'll feel far more suspicious about what you are likely to be saying behind his back.

If you have lied to your child in the past—or spread negative comments about her to others—confess your behavior to her and ask her forgiveness. Wipe the slate clean between you, and move forward. Be determined to win your child's trust and confidence by communicating in an honest, truthful, and positive way with her and about her.

46 ❝ Will You Ever Send Me Away?

If your child voices this question, take it seriously. Here are several other ways your child might phrase this question:

- Are you sorry that I am your child?

- Do you wish you had never given birth to me (or adopted me)?

- Would you rather I was someone else (perhaps a sibling or a perceived "favorite" child)?

The fear underlying these questions tends to be rooted in a child's perception of himself and his conclusion that, for some reason, he isn't "good enough" for your love.

No Conditions on Love Are you placing conditions on your child's love—saying, for example, "If you do such and so, Mommy will give you a hug," or "Daddy doesn't like a boy who does this and that"? If so, don't. Your child needs to feel that you love her and that you will always love her, regardless of her behavior.

Your child needs to feel that he is loved solely because he is *your* child—not because you *have* to love him but because you are privileged to do so and take delight in doing so.

No Comparisons   Don't compare your child to others. Love the uniqueness of your child, and delight in *her* accomplishments, *her* special traits and abilities, *her* opinions and ideas. Your child is her own person.

In applauding the success of one child—perhaps a child who is not even in your family—be sensitive to the fact that a child who hears your applause may feel he is being rejected or criticized as part of the process. Avoid saying, "I'm sure that the winner's parents love him a great deal," or "Everybody loves a success," or "See . . . that's what happens when you try hard." Instead, say simply, "He did a good job," and leave it at that. No comparisons. No innuendos of a hope for similar achievement from your child. No blame laid at your child's feet for his *not* winning or achieving.

No "Favorites"   Many a child has felt what Dick Smothers frequently says to his brother, Tom, in his comedy routine: "Mom always liked you best." Although you may have a greater innate understanding of one child's personality over another or find that one child responds in ways more like your own responses, you can make a *choice* to love each of your children equally.

Be careful not to play favorites. Don't defend one

child more than another or show more affection to one child. Be fair with your children. If you feel a lack of love for one child, ask God to give you a bit of His supernatural love for that child.

Blended Families This matter of being sent away or loved less is an especially critical one for blended families to address. Stepchildren and half siblings frequently perceive inequities. Do your best to play by the same rules with all the children in your household. Don't allow one child, or one group of children, to take center stage at all times, to receive all the rewards or punishment, or to be included in more activities with parents. Talk about feelings openly. Don't let perceived inequities or injustices stew to the boiling point.

Talk About It Let your child know—by directly saying so—that you wouldn't trade her for the world. Pull your child close from time to time and say, "I'm hugging the greatest kid ever!" or "I'm so grateful that God has allowed me to be a part of your life."

47 ☾ Will I Ever Get Big?

Days and months and years move by slowly for a child. Sometimes a child tends to feel stuck at a stage, and insecurity and frustration can develop that result in these questions:

- Will I ever be smarter?

- Will I ever get better at this?

- Will I ever be allowed to do this by myself?

- Will I ever be given permission to go?

The frustration is rooted in current dissatisfaction with her abilities or another's trust level. A wise parent will recognize and address both concerns.

Don't Emphasize Lack of Ability A child hears "you're too young," "not now," and "someday" more than he can count. Avoid these responses whenever possible! Instead, point to a level of ability that is required for the event or activity in question, and let your child know that you will do your best to help him develop that ability or reach that point of maturity.

- Say, "To be able to go on that ride, you need to be able to touch the floor with your feet so you can brace yourself. You'll get there!"

- Say, "Before you can do that, you need to know how to read. Let's keep rehearsing the alphabet and sounding out words and you'll be reading before you know it!"

- Say, "You can do that once I see that you know how to do certain things," and then name those things.

Whenever possible, point toward intermediate steps that your child can or will take toward a goal.

Point Out Progress   Cite your child's past improvement and current level of accomplishment when holding out a level of ability that is required for a future activity or event. Give your child a sense that she is on the right track and that she is moving toward the level at which permission might be granted or success achieved. Avoid changing the scale midway through the course.

Avoid Setting Age Levels   Don't tell your eight-year-old child he can go at the age of twelve. In the first place, that will seem like an eternity away. In the second place, he may *not* be mature enough to go at twelve, or he may be mature enough to go at ten!

Anticipate Your Child's Maturity Assure your child that you believe she will one day grow up and that when she does, she will be a successful, faithful, generous, loving, and healthy human being. Never squelch a child's dream about her future. Even if you think she will never be, earn, win, or experience what she envisions, don't put down her dream. Instead, focus your encouragement on the traits that you desire to see in your child—a robust love for God, a generous love for others, and a healthy love of self.

Trust Much of what a parent allows a child to do is related to the degree that a parent trusts a child. Talk often to your child about the importance that you place on

- honesty. Require your child to tell you the truth and to face life squarely.

- good judgment. Look for ways in which your child is growing in his ability to tell right from wrong and to make wise choices that will bring benefit to all concerned. Applaud acts and decisions that portray wisdom and forethought.

- consistency of behavior and belief. Let your child know that before you can trust her out of your sight, you are looking for consistency of behavior and belief—that she treats all people with respect and courtesy, that she is able to control her temper and channel her anger into productive and positive behavior no matter the provocation, and that she is willing to accept direction, guidance, and discipline.

48 (What If I Die?

As a child matures, he inevitably encounters death —often a beloved grandparent's death or the death of a pet. In the grieving process, a child frequently asks, "Will I die, too?" or "What will happen to me when I die?"

Never lie to your child about death—saying that your child will never die or that you won't die. Death is a fact of every person's existence. At the same time, you can hold out to your child the *hope of life*—that your child will grow up to be a healthy adult who will live out her full life span with an enjoyable quality of life and fulfilling work.

You can also hold out to your child the hope of *eternal* life—that you anticipate your child will go to heaven when he dies and that he will be loved and nurtured there. Talk about what heaven is like. Let your child imagine the fun and joy of life in heaven.

Speak to your child about death being a change for the better. Your child's new body will be one that never gets sick and never experiences pain. She will be able to do things with a heavenly body that she can't do on earth.

Don't Belabor the Point Answer your child's questions about death to the extent that your child wants an answer. (Don't tell him how to make a clock if he wants to know only what time it is!) For some children, the answer, "You aren't going to die today, so let's live today," may suffice. For others, the answer, "You'll go to heaven and be with Grandma and Grandpa and God until I join you there," may be suitable. Be open to your child's questions and field them the best you can, but don't offer more information than he seeks.

Discuss Terminal Illness If your child has been diagnosed with a serious illness that may be terminal, assure her that you will be there for her, loving her and standing by her regardless what happens. Talk over the situation with your doctor and your clergyperson before talking directly to your child about death.

Help Your Child Prepare for Eternity Talk to your child about God in terms that your child understands. Teach him about a loving, eternal God who understands all things, including what is right and helpful for your child, and who desires to give your child everything that will be for his benefit and eternal joy. Explain that God's will is not always done on this earth—that evil and people's wills sometimes get in the way of what God desires to do—but that God's will is *always* done in heaven. That's why your child can count on heaven being wonderful!

Prepare your child to live in right relationship with God, now and forever. Your child is a spiritual being from the moment she is born. She is capable of praise and worship long before she has any sense of right and wrong. Join with your child in praising God. Make songs of thanksgiving and worship some of the first songs your child learns. Let your child grow up feeling comfortable with God. She'll fear death far less.

49 ⟨ Will You Always Be Able to Forgive Me?

Children often feel a great sense of insecurity and fear after doing, saying, or even thinking something that they believe is unforgivable. Children can and do feel guilt.

Alleviate Guilt   Don't let your child suffer under its burden. Here are some ways you can help your child deal with guilt.

Teach your child the difference between an accident and a willful act   Accidents aren't sins. Only acts of the will are sins. It isn't a sin that your child knocks over Aunt Sally's vase when he gestures as he walks by the end table. It is wrong, however, if he takes Aunt Sally's vase outside and sets it up on a wall for target practice with a baseball!

Teach your child how to get rid of guilt   Being truly sorry for the deed (and not just sorry that she got caught), asking for forgiveness, and changing her behavior (as an act of her will) to do what is right are involved in getting rid of guilt.

Teach your child the difference between regret, an apology, and a request for forgiveness Regret is saying, "I'm sorry it happened" (which usually means, "I'm sorry I messed up," or "I'm sorry I got caught"). An apology is saying, "I'm sorry for the pain or injury I caused you." A request for forgiveness is saying, "I'm sorry. Please forgive me for hurting you." A request for forgiveness is the only act to which the hurting party can truly respond with the will. Your child should ask for forgiveness to let the other person free your child from her heart.

Teach your child to ask both God's forgiveness and forgiveness from the person she has hurt, injured, and/or betrayed Let your child know that when she asks for forgiveness, God always grants it. (Help your child memorize 1 John 1:9: "If we confess our sins, He is faithful and just to forgive us our sins and to cleanse us from all unrighteousness.")

If your child asks forgiveness of another person who refuses to grant forgiveness, tell your child that he has done all that is required by God in asking for forgiveness. The refusal by the other person becomes the other person's problem, not your child's.

Asking another person for forgiveness is sometimes difficult. Agree to go with your child as she asks if it will help her have the courage to face the person she has wronged.

Let your child know that forgiveness doesn't always erase consequences   Your child can be truly repentant and truly forgiven, yet he must still pay for Aunt Sally's broken vase.

Assure your child that no sin is beyond God's ability to forgive or your desire to forgive   In being a forgiving person, you are showing your child how to forgive, and you are also freeing your child to seek out forgiveness.

Freely Forgive   When your child asks your forgiveness, freely and quickly forgive—without qualifications.

Encourage your child freely to forgive those who ask for *her* forgiveness. The healthy and secure child knows that she stands in right relationship with others. Forgiveness is the key.

50 ❝ Hold Out the Hope of a Better Tomorrow

Children join adults in feeling at times as if the present *is* the future—that things will never change, never get better, never cease to be painful or awkward.

Hold out to your child the hope of a brighter tomorrow!

Almost anybody can endure just about anything if the person knows that the pain, distress, or discomfort is "but for a short season." When a person begins to view all of life, however, as being filled with hurting moments, that person quickly begins to fear life itself. He is likely to develop very poor self-esteem and to feel inadequate or uneasy about doing even the simplest tasks. The person who expects something bad—or worse—to happen around every bend of life's road lives in insecurity.

Optimistic Approach Be your child's voice of optimism.

Believe in your child's potential.

Talk about the future you believe is possible for your child. Be realistic, but be hopeful. Believe for the best.

Don't get bogged down in the current problem. Be objective about the problem, and help your child analyze the situation, map out a course of action, and start taking steps to improve the circumstance, learn the unlearned material, or heal the relationship.

The Promise of Change   Point out ways in which life changes—the seasons, for example, or the way in which your child has grown physically during the last year. To a child, a day seems like a year, a year like an eternity. Help your child see that changes have occurred in her life and thus will continue to occur.

Express to your child that you regard each day as having new promise—that you consider each day to be a new beginning. Rejoice in his successful days. When days aren't successful, remind him of past successful days, and anticipate future successful days with him. Let your child know that you believe "happy days will come again."

Prolonged Depression   If your child seems depressed over a period of time, consider taking her for professional counseling. Even children experience mental depression. And sometimes prolonged depression is a sign of an illness or a chemical deficiency.

51 ☾ Faith and Prayer

Assure your child that he is never alone in life—no matter how alone he might feel, and no matter the circumstances he faces. He has a heavenly Father who sees his every move, hears his every cry, and responds to his every prayer.

The child who truly feels she has an ally in God is a child who *feels* an inner strength that transcends all situations and relationships.

Faith Teach your child three things about God.

1. God is your heavenly Father, and He knows what is happening to you Nothing escapes God's notice —not a scraped knee, a harsh word from a teacher, or a lost teddy bear.

2. God is your loving Father, and He cares about you God feels sorrow when your child hurts, and He rejoices when she is happy and safe.

3. God is your eternal Father, and He has a plan for your "forever best" God's desires for your child are the highest and best—beyond what you, your child, or anyone can imagine. God's will for your child is sometimes limited by your child's will and the willful acts of others, but it is God's desire that your child love Him and be with Him for all eternity.

These are the cornerstones on which your child's faith will be built. Establish them early in his life.

Prayer Talk frequently about the availability and accessibility of God. Teach your child to talk to God on her own—tell her that she *can* talk to God about anything, at any time, in any place, and that God will hear her prayer.

Why pray about what God already knows? Because God desires to communicate with us. He wants to develop a talking-and-walking relationship with us. Don't limit your child's prayer time to requests. Spend time in praise and worship with your child.

The child who knows in his heart that God is only a prayer away has immediate access to His supernatural security, confidence, and strength.

52 ❛ The Power of Love

No matter how secure a child feels in himself, or in his faith that God is on his side, he will never feel completely secure unless he knows that you love him with a lasting and unconditional love.

Great Love   Tell your child often that you love him. Say directly, "I love you."

Let your child know that your love for her is without qualification; rather, it flows simply from the fact that your child exists and that you are in relationship with your child!

Let your child know that there's nothing he can do to destroy your love or diminish it. That doesn't mean you will always approve or applaud your child's actions—or cover for his mistakes—but even in moments of your child's sin, failure, or error, you will love him.

Great Value   Ultimately, your child's happiness, security, and courage aren't linked to circumstances. A child can feel secure in her heart and in her value as a person, no matter what happens around her or to her at the hands of peers or enemies. Her security and courage are rooted in the way she feels about herself, and the way she feels about herself is drawn almost entirely from the way she perceives that you feel about her. When your child feels your unconditional love, she loves and values herself.

A child who is secure in the love of a parent experiences far fewer moments of trauma, uneasiness, or paralyzing fear.

Great Potential   Give your child open and frequent expressions of your love. In so doing, you'll be giving your child the security he desperately needs to be able to take risks in life and to reach his full potential as a human being.